HOW TO PAINT
COLOUR & LIGHT
IN WATERCOLOUR

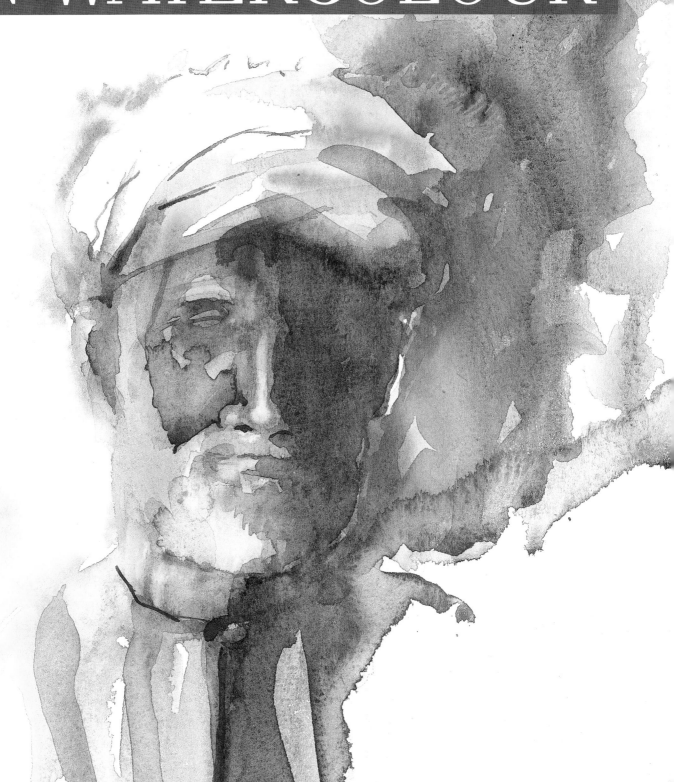

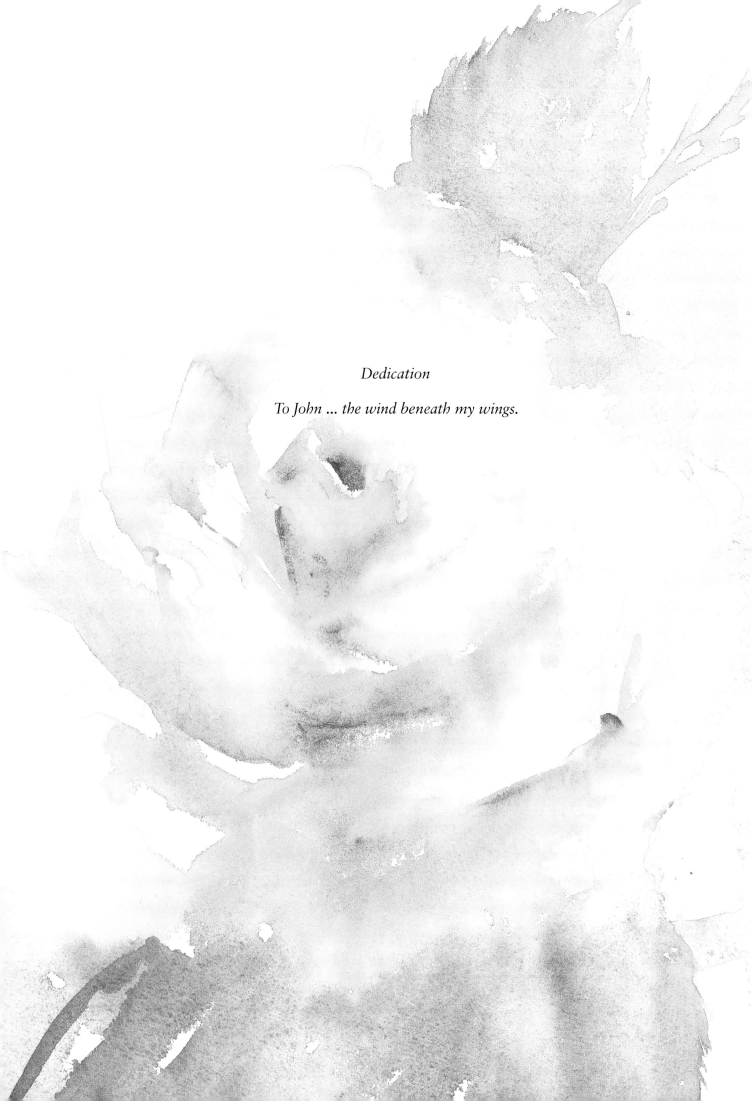

Dedication

To John ... the wind beneath my wings.

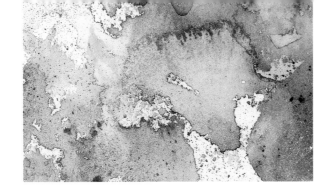

HOW TO PAINT
COLOUR & LIGHT
IN WATERCOLOUR

JEAN HAINES

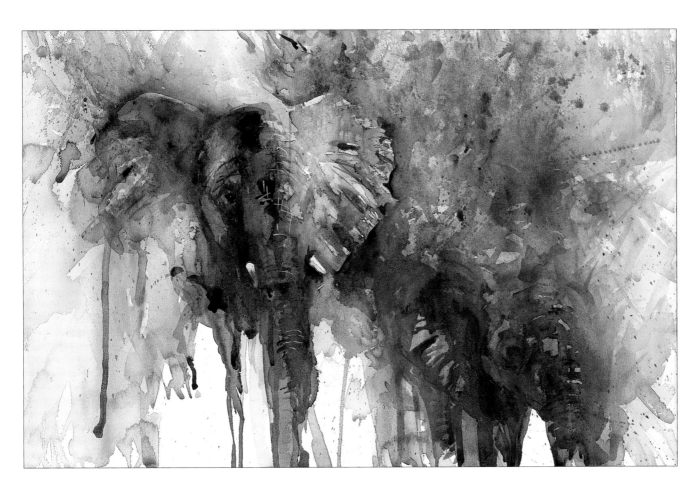

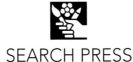

SEARCH PRESS

First published in Great Britain 2010

Search Press Limited
Wellwood, North Farm Road,
Tunbridge Wells, Kent TN2 3DR

Text copyright © Jean Haines 2010

Photographs by Roddy Paine Photographic Studio

Photographs and design copyright © Search Press Ltd 2010

ISBN: 978-1-84448-488-1

The Publishers and author can accept no responsibility for any
consequences arising from the information, advice or instructions given
in this publication.

Suppliers

If you have difficulty in obtaining any of the materials and equipment
mentioned in the book, please visit www.winsornewton.com.

Publishers' note

All the step-by-step photographs in this book feature the author,
Jean Haines, demonstrating painting in watercolour. No models have
been used.

Printed in Malaysia.

Cover
Beauty of Venice
71 x 61cm (28 x 24in)

Page 1
Wisdom, Dubai
46 x 56cm (18 x 22in)

Page 3
Out of Africa
71 x 61cm (28 x 24in)

Acknowledgements

*The Society For All Artists (SAA) recognised
my passion for watercolour, introduced me to
writing articles for* Paint *magazine and from
here the feedback from SAA members urged me
to write and fulfil my ambition to become an
author. Chandy Rogers, John Hope Hawkins
and Richard Hope Hawkins of SAA all led me to
a wonderful opportunity to write my first book.
I know they all play a part in many artists'
careers. To have this opportunity to say thank
you is a privilege.*

*Search Press as a publisher made my dream
come true. The whole team at this wonderful
company have to be seen to be believed. I owe
very special gratitude to Roz Dace, Editorial
Director, whose faith in me from the very
beginning of this project has been incredible.
Katie Sparkes, my editor, has a wonderful
personality and nature, understanding how I
wanted my book to emerge and at times almost
feeling as if she knew me inside out.*

*Amazing photographers, Roddy Paine and
Gavin Sawyer – thank you for making my
first photography shoot memorable, fun and a
fantastic experience.*

*To every artist and student who has encouraged
me to write my first book in watercolour I owe
this book. Your enthusiasm has led me to this
stage in my art career and I cannot thank you
enough for all your enthusiasm and interest in
my work. I have taken every comment on board
and hope you enjoy what you have wished me to
do for some time now. This book is for you.*

*Finally I owe a huge thank you to my wonderful
husband John who not only always encourages
me to follow my dreams but has a hand in every
one that has come true. In this case, allowing
me the time and space to complete my
first book.*

*Thank you.
Jean Haines*

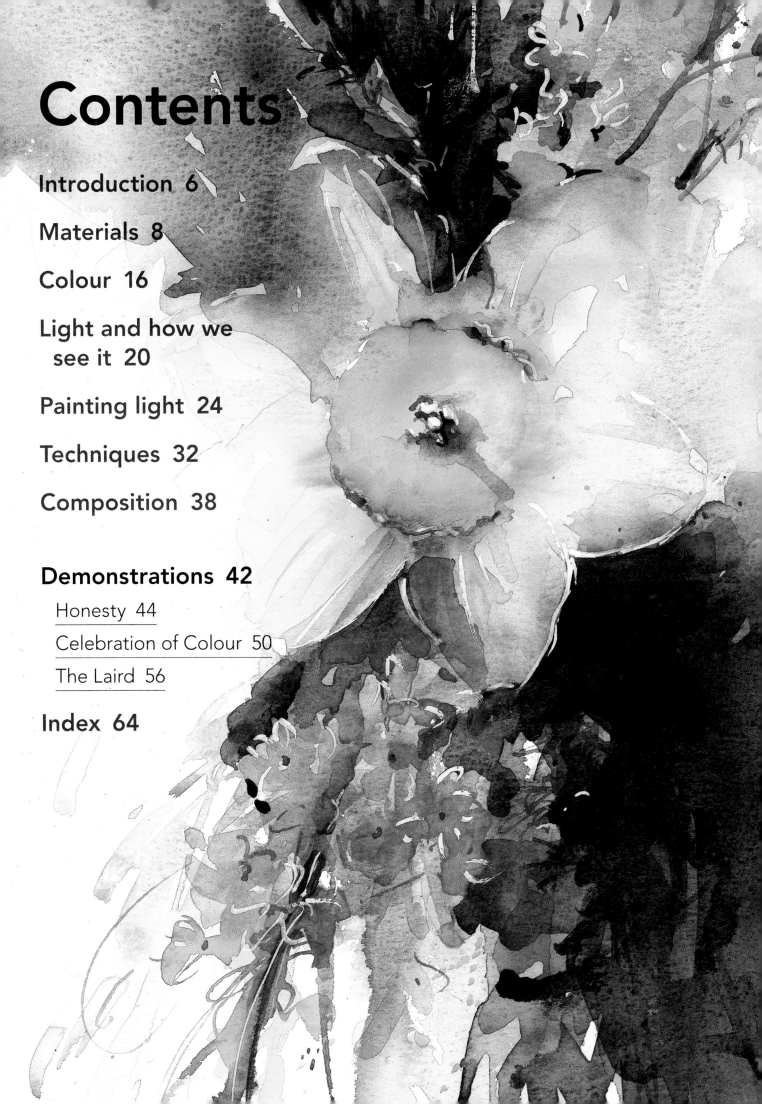

Contents

Introduction

I first saw a pure violet-coloured shadow when I was living in Dubai. I remember looking in awe as the sunlight hit one side of a dishdash, the white robes worn by Arab men, leaving warm shades of gold splattered amongst the violet shadow cast on the ground at the market. Everywhere I turned sunlight created patterns of colour all around me and I was fascinated.

For years I had looked at watercolour paintings depicting scenes where violet or other colours were used to depict shadows, but I had never truly noticed colour so strongly as at that moment in time. It was as though a veil had been removed from my eyes and all of a sudden different colours came into play as I looked at other subjects I had often painted. I saw green in faces for the very first time and a whole host of colours other than blue in a sky.

Suddenly, picking up a paintbrush became an addiction as I constantly tried to capture the play of light in each scene that unfolded before my eyes: sunflowers in France, fish markets in Hong Kong, carnival masks in Venice, camels and mosques in Dubai. I have travelled and lived in many countries since 1989, and have continually met wonderful artists who have shared their knowledge with me and students who have asked me questions regarding light and the best way to paint it. My reply is always filled with enthusiasm and excitement for the fact that they can see light in a scene in the first place. This, to me, was the hardest part in my watercolour journey – actually seeing colour and light.

I hope my book on how to paint colour and light in watercolour takes you to a stage in your art journey where you too start to see violet shadows and colour in a way that leads you into a whole new world as an artist. And I hope my addiction to light and colour becomes a passion for you as much as it is for me.

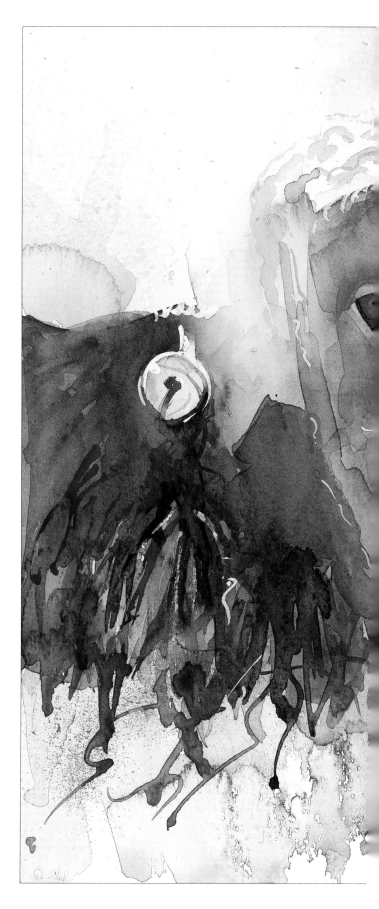

Venetian Mask
71 x 61cm (28 x 24in)
The subject is only slightly off centre with contrasts of colour either side of the mask making use of watermarks for added effects.

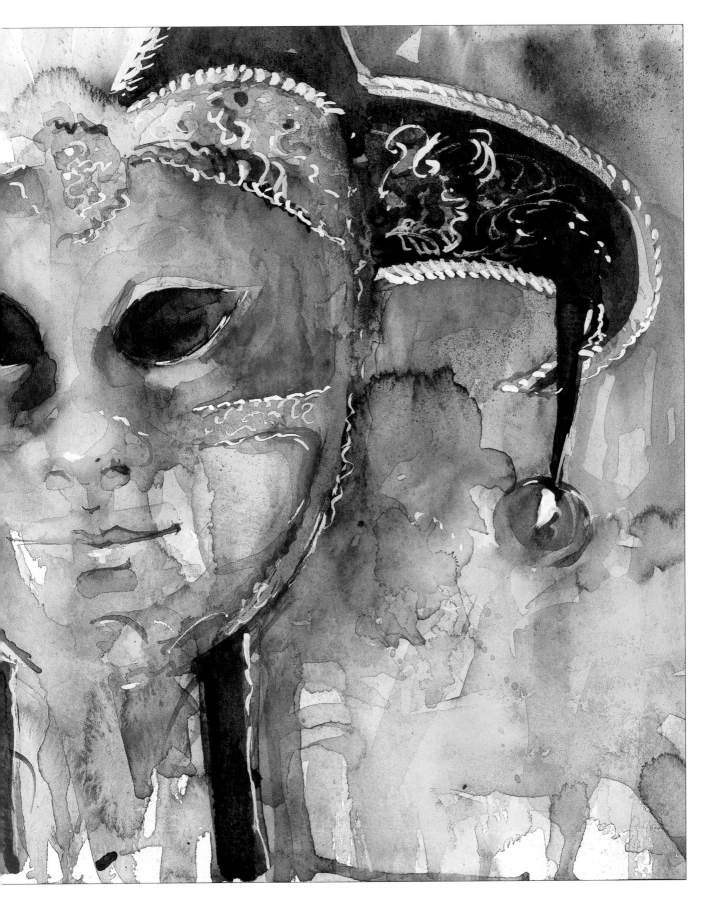

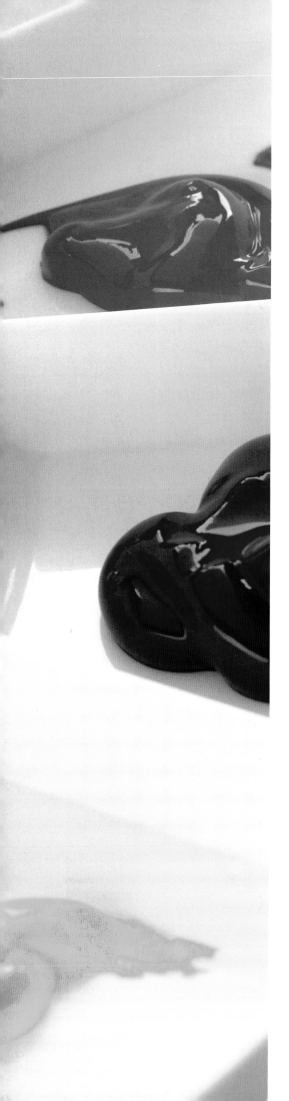

Materials

Looking into an artist's studio is like a window into their soul. An insight into how they think, work and create. I have an Aladdin's cave which I venture into with new treasure, whether it is a new subject to paint, collected from a morning walk, or something new to apply pigment with!

Over time my collection of materials has grown, but in it are some very special friends that I couldn't live without. Items I reach for automatically; brushes that work well for me; favourite colours. If I were stranded on a desert island, these are what I would grab to survive with.

As artists we need paper, colour, palette and brushes plus a water container. The items we use will evolve over time as we develop different techniques covering a variety of styles within the magical medium of watercolour. We grow as artists, and our collection of materials grows too.

Water

For me the most important resource I work with is water, and lots of it. Small containers do not suit my style and I need a constant supply of clean, fresh water at hand. For this reason I often have a number of containers on my art desk and a huge jug of clean water to refill them as I work during the day. Clear containers are excellent for showing when your water needs changing. Always work with two so that one can hold clean water to prepare for loading your brush with fresh pigment while the other can be used for cleaning your brushes in between shade selections.

 Tip
You are aiming to achieve watercolours that literally sing with colour and light. Always work with clean water for the very best results as this will ensure you achieve fresh vibrant colours. Using muddy water at any stage will affect your results and could lose the effect of light that you are desperately trying to gain.

Try making a few brushstrokes with discoloured water and see how your paper is affected. This will give you an idea of how fresh pigment can be dulled by dirty water.

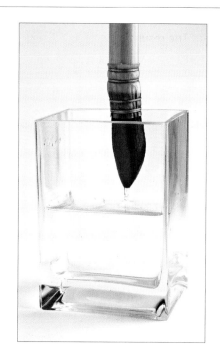

Paper

I have painted in watercolour on many surfaces over the years. Not always watercolour paper either, as one of my favourite collections is of Arab faces painted on antique crumpled paper found in an old warehouse while on my travels. In fact I have painted with tea, coffee, wine or anything that was available to capture my subjects. I would grab the first piece of any kind of paper that I could find suitable to work on and cover it in studies that caught my eye at that moment in time.

This is why carrying a sketchbook with you and some basic watercolour equipment is invaluable. Regularly taking notes on colour and form and making sketches train your eye and improve your drawing skills. This makes you into a better artist, and can lead to superb paintings in your studio at a later date based on the records you keep in your sketchbook.

Over the years I have experimented with many kinds of paper surfaces. I've discovered the best paper to work with is dictated by both the subject of the painting and the technique used. What I aim for in my work is a gentle flow of water carrying the pigment, and this is far easier if I choose at the beginning of each project a suitable surface to aid my results. When you are learning or trying out new techniques, it is wise to use reasonably priced paper because many of your pieces may end up in the bin. But as you grow as an artist, you will discover which paper gives you the very best results for your chosen subject and technique.

Paper surfaces can be broken down into two main groups: smooth and rough. Smooth surfaces are wonderful for still-life subjects, or flowers with soft silky petals such as poppies that can be enhanced by colours gliding over the paper. I also enjoy working with rough paper because I adore how the pigment sits in the pockets formed by the texture on the surface. Granulation and colour fusions are aided, allowing colours to merge in some sections and simply sit in others.

Even as a beginner, it is vital to use good quality watercolour paper. You cannot get an idea of how pigment dries or flows if the paper you are using is of an inferior quality. Always work with paper no less than 300gsm (140lb) weight.

Painting using a granular pigment on rough paper (left), and transparent colour on smooth paper (right). The results are very different.

Tip
The more water you use in your painting, the heavier the paper needs to be.

Brushes and painting knives

Choice of brush is very personal to many artists. We all have our favourite brushes, and many artists possess large numbers of brushes that they have bought over the years and that have been a 'must have' at one stage or another in their career. The most important thing this experience has taught me is that the best quality brushes really do help me achieve better results, and are far more enjoyable to use.

From travelling and living abroad for so long I have amassed a vast collection of brushes. My favourites are Chinese brushes, given to me by my Chinese teacher while I was living and studying watercolour in Asia. I also still have the very first brushes I bought years ago when I was tempted to buy the latest trends in 'must-have' accessories. This latter collection is doomed to a brush pot that is now purely for show. I sometimes take this into my workshops just to show my students how much money you can waste in an art shop when you don't know what you are doing. I look at the brushes I use now as if they are my best friends. I look after them and I have owned some for a very long time.

My favourite brushes, which I have used for all the demonstrations in this book, are shown below. I also use a painting knife (no. 2 in the picture below). A very large brush, such as a pure squirrel pointed wash brush, size 8 (brush no. 1 in the picture) is ideal for large washes and working on large pieces of paper. It is vital that your brush loads well and holds a lot of water, especially if you are trying the techniques in this book. I also recommend the Winsor & Newton Kolinsky sable range of brushes in several sizes: a size 3 fine rigger (brush no. 4) for dropping small amounts of colour into sections of your washes, and a size 10 (brush no. 3) for main subject work are invaluable.

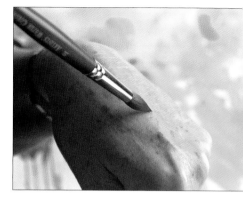

How you choose your brush is interesting. Try brushing the sable tip against the back of your hand. Feel how soft it is and think about the light pressure you are using. Always use this gentle pressure when working so you don't disturb the surface of the paper.

Tip

Use the best quality brushes you can afford. If you look after them well they will last you a very long time and be a wise investment, especially if you love painting. Cheaper brushes tend to lose hair and their fine-point tip, and often split. Never leave your brushes standing in water, and store them upright, with the heads uppermost, in clean, dry, open containers.

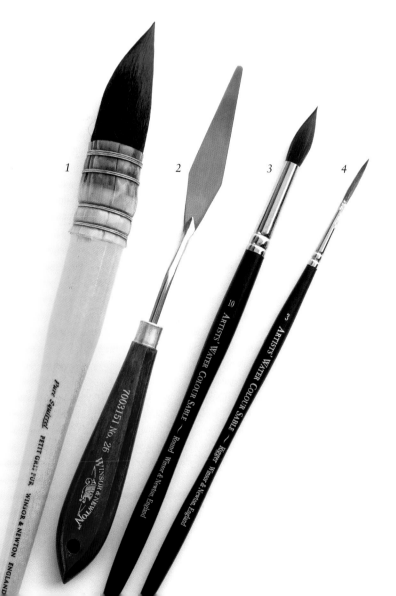

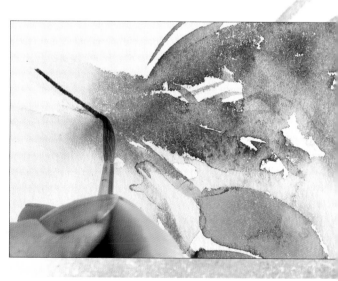

Why choose sable brushes?

Sable brushes load well, which is vital to enable pigment to be carried over the paper. They have flexible heads, which allows free and flowing movement of the brush. This encourages exciting and varied brushstrokes that, importantly, add interest and impact to your watercolours.

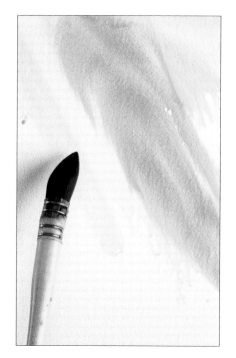

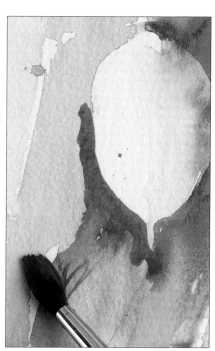

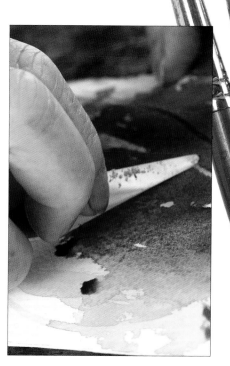

Use a large brush to place washes of colour. Load the brush with a combination of pigment and water and apply with a variety of confident brushstrokes. These brushes are superb for covering large sections of paper, especially background washes.

Use a medium-sized brush for medium detail. This brush is extremely versatile – use it to paint in curved strokes, and to bleed paint diagonally across the painting. You can produce finer strokes using the point of the brush, and broader strokes by dragging the edge of the brush sideways across the painting.

When using bold and almost dry applications of pigment it is possible to draw fine directional lines through the colour to create textural lines. A small painting knife is ideal for this kind of detail. Please be aware that the surface of the paper should never be ruined by heavy-handed use of this technique. Light touches are vital.

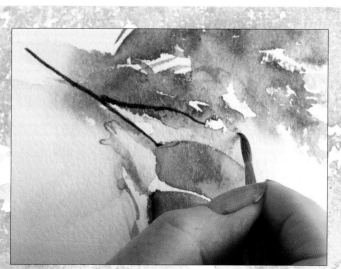

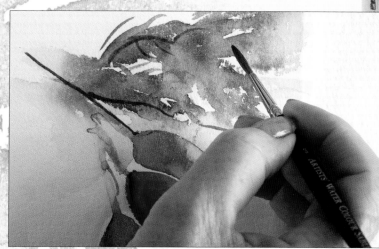

Use a small brush for small strokes. Hold the brush near the tip for more controlled work.

Palette

White palettes are wonderful because they give you an idea of the colour of the pigment on white paper. Keeping the mixing area of your palette clean will ensure you always have vibrant, fresh colour in your paintings.

Choosing a palette is a very personal decision, and there are many to choose from. I sometimes mix my colours on paper, and sometimes on the palette. I use a lot of water for soft, whispery washes, so for my technique it is vital to use a palette that has deep wells to contain large amounts of colour and a large area for mixing.

I own a collection of palettes so that I can keep shades for the vast variety of my subjects separate. Portraits, landscapes and flowers all require a different selection of colours. Having a tried-and-tested set of colours to work with helps when I am working on larger paintings, as I can then focus on the subject rather than on what colours to use.

I prefer to work with tubes of colour rather than pans and I buy the largest available in my favourite shades. These I empty into my palette, in quantities dictated by the amount I wish to use. These are never tiny dots of colour; they are always huge, delicious, juicy quantities that I find appealing, and which entice me to use them. Get into the habit of placing colour on to your palette and working with it – paint is always far more attractive once squeezed out of the tube. Colour left unused for months is like that outfit you once bought for best but never wore, or the savings you have put away for a rainy day – always there but never enjoyed. Use lots of colour and have fun with it!

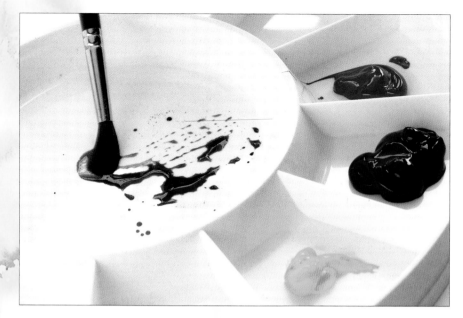

Don't try to work with tiny dots of colour on your palette. Enjoy and celebrate using colour from the minute you squeeze it from the tube!

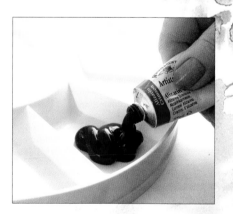

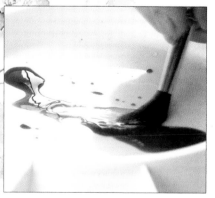

Don't be afraid to squeeze out large quantities of colour into the wells of your palette, and mix your colours confidently using plenty of clean water in the mixing area.

Watercolour

To achieve a painting that positively sings with colour and light, it is essential to use a watercolour range that is excellent. The properties of each shade, because of the pigment in its make-up, will either add to or detract from your results. There could be nothing worse than buying wonderful brushes and paper and then producing a dull result. To achieve vibrant paintings with colours that are full of life, always buy the best products and learn to use them well.

When I studied art in China I was given a small piece of ochre by my Chinese art mentor. I was asked to grind the pigment from it on an ink stone. When mixed with water it created the most vibrant natural shade of yellow ochre and I fell in love with the brilliance immediately. My Chinese teacher told me how, in her youth, she had to mix every single colour by hand before she could paint. Her teachers would instruct her and she would learn how to choose and use colour wisely.

To be able to buy ready-mixed pigment today is a luxury we often take for granted. We don't have to forage for natural substances that stain or last. Over the years, manufacturers have created wonderful paints for serious artists, and as my painting depends highly on interaction between shades, I avoid inferior products. For the same fresh brilliance and excitement I obtained from the yellow ochre given to me by my teacher in China, I choose from the Winsor & Newton watercolour range, which offers both superb quality and an exciting range of colours.

The colours shown opposite are all of the colours I have used for the projects in this book, and represent a good basic palette for a variety of subjects. You will also find I use burnt umber at times to introduce darker shades when necessary.

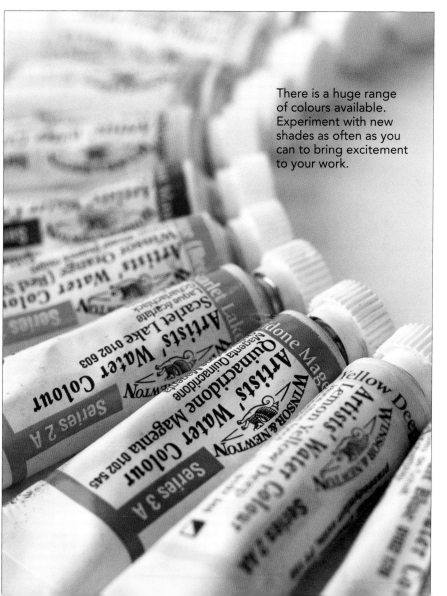

There is a huge range of colours available. Experiment with new shades as often as you can to bring excitement to your work.

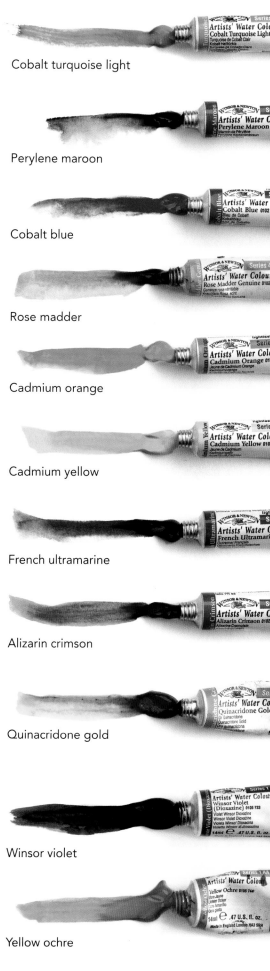

Cobalt turquoise light

Perylene maroon

Cobalt blue

Rose madder

Cadmium orange

Cadmium yellow

French ultramarine

Alizarin crimson

Quinacridone gold

Winsor violet

Yellow ochre

13

Other useful items

Paper, water, colour and brushes are the main materials for most artists, but in art studios all over the world you will often find other additions to the artist's collection of working equipment. Here are a few treasures to be found in my own studio.

Easel

I often work standing up at an easel for larger paintings. This gives me freedom to move my arms, which avoids tight, controlled brushstrokes. When working for long periods of time a table easel is ideal for allowing me to paint comfortably seated when adding fine detail and finishing touches.

Whatever I am painting, my paper will be at a similar angle to the subject so that I can capture the positions of the features, light and shadows accurately. Working in this way will automatically give you a good start to achieving a better result. Finding an easel that can be used at a variety of angles is a wonderful asset when working with watercolour. At times, you will need to allow the pigments time to evolve during their drying process. At different stages you will see magical effects. Only time and patience will give you an insight into what is possible with this wonderful medium.

Salt

I find salt invaluable for creating incredible patterns, such as the painting *Sunflower Explosion* shown opposite.

Inks

Sometimes in a painting I will add a touch of ink to a tiny section. The contrast often amazes me. I find bold sections can add impact by contrasting against softer areas of colour in a composition. These dramatic touches need to be applied sparingly as the beauty of traditional and transparent watercolour is in its translucent quality. To destroy that beauty is almost like losing part of the lyrics to a song.

Gouache

When you have lost the white of the paper, touches of white gouache can bring a painting to life. Try a small dot in the highlight of an eye or just on the edge of one petal to add drama.

Imagination

I have a small box containing pieces of card and twigs that I have collected over time and which I use in my paintings, from time to time, to create interesting effects. I often use card to paint against to create straight edges of buildings or even vases. I rarely sketch prior to painting, so having some means to hand of achieving straight lines is a great help. I also use card in a similar way to the painting knife (see page 14).

There are many tricks and tips like these that lead to interesting paintings. Always be on the look-out for your next resource that could lead to a new technique or effect. Just about anything can be used to bring a painting to life and prompt the viewer to ask, 'How on earth did the artist achieve that?'. Most artists wish to achieve unique results, so unique techniques are a good place to start.

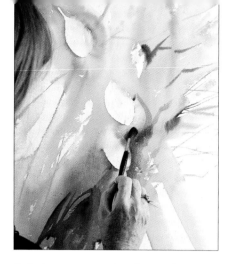

Painting at an angle allows pigment to be carried by water, which will flow when drying. This creates interest and wonderful effects.

Sunflower Explosion
71 x 61cm (28 x 24in)
Salt was applied to the initial first wash while it was still slightly damp. I love this result so much I haven't even added further detail.

Play with a variety of objects and see what patterns you can create. Never dismiss any idea that could give you a new effect. Finding that inner child from years ago, who would eagerly experiment and enjoy playing with colour and patterns, could see you inventing a fabulous new way of working that no one has yet discovered. Make time to be a five-year-old again. Get that freedom and feeling of spontaneous creativity back into your life and your painting. It will show in your results – and in your face – as your imagination comes alive. You may even find yourself smiling more often while you paint.

Tip
Have fun and invent your own texture ideas.

Patience

Wouldn't it be wonderful if we could find an endless supply of patience, so that we would never again race our work or attempt to carry on painting when we should be taking time to decide what is needed in a picture or even whether the painting is actually finished or not. Reading through my materials again I must admit I now can't wait to experiment with washes and texture effects, so I'm going to look at colour next, and the ways in which we can use it.

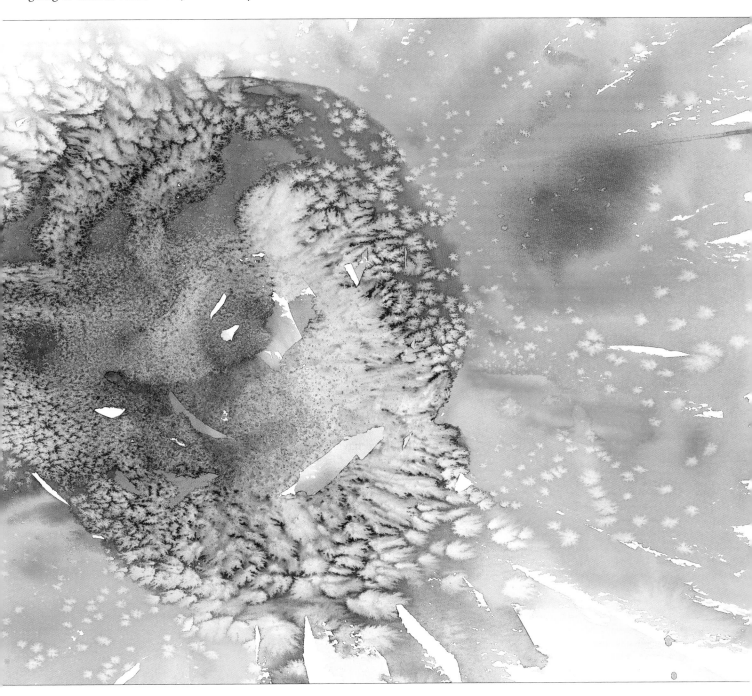

Colour

I cannot imagine a world without colour. Every day our lives are enriched by what we see, from the minute we wake to the end of the day. The sights around us change with the light from morning to night. How we see colour and how we paint it is a wonderful part of being an artist. Knowing how pigment works so that you can choose the right shade to portray a given subject is also a vital part in working with watercolour as a medium.

   Although there are many books available on colour theory, this section covers everything you need to know about how to use colour in your paintings. My practical approach means that from the moment you start reading you will need to pick up a paintbrush and start playing with paint to encourage creative colour mixing for paintings with a more interesting and original appearance. So let's get started!

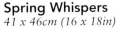

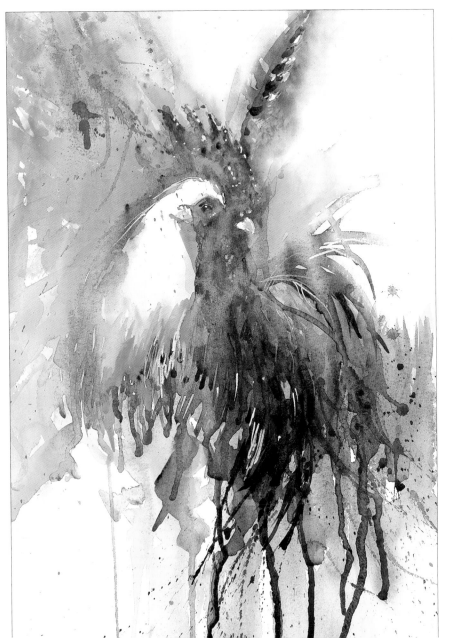

Spring Whispers
41 x 46cm (16 x 18in)

> ## Tip
> It takes time to understand colour: how it can improve a simple painting and how it can add to a brilliant result. Time taken reading this section will be enormously beneficial to improving your own work.

King of All He Sees
46 x 56cm (18 x 22in)

Three primary colours

To begin you will need a good quality watercolour paper and a clean white palette. Starting with the three primary colours, you can learn how mixing can provide a vast number of shades suitable for the projects later in this book. I have chosen alizarin crimson, cadmium yellow and cobalt blue. For the first exercise I would like you to place a small amount of pigment of each colour in a circle on the paper, starting with alizarin crimson. Next to this, with a clean brush, place a track of clean water leading away from the circle but not touching it. Then, with a clean brush, gently touch the circle of pigment and sit back to watch what happens. Observation will improve your knowledge of working with this magical medium. The pigment will gently flow into the wet section of the paper, but not move to the dry sections. Also notice the beautiful transparent colour that is in the diluted area. Do not be tempted to touch the colour or water at this stage. Allow the water and pigment to work alone. Now try this simple exercise again with both cadmium yellow and cobalt blue.

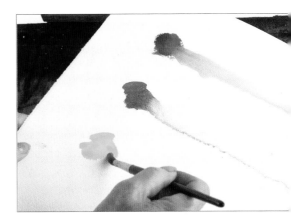

This first exercise, which I have described opposite, is the best way to start understanding how colour works.

Whispers and shouts

The gentle colour you see in the flow of the water track in this first exercise I refer to as a 'whisper'. This contrasts with the bold, almost dry, circular application of pigment that I refer to as a 'shout'. In any painting you will find a mixture of whispers and shouts, which contrast and add interest. See *Spring Whispers* in contrast to the vibrant cockerel painting on the opposite page.

Water and colour

It is interesting to note how water plays a vital role in this exercise. Without it the pigment would not flow. This is why we work with water *and* colour. Never underestimate how important it is to learn how to add the correct amount of water for any given effect. Many artists comment that watercolour is difficult to use as a medium, but if you really understand the beauty of its nature your paintings will always be fascinating – not only in their finished state, but while you are creating them also.

Brilliant primary colours are often used in subjects such as flowers or still life. Transparent, watery mixtures are more commonly used in landscapes, portraits and animal paintings, with results that look highly professional and advanced in technique.

Try this

Try repeating this exercise with different primary colours, for example cerulean blue, cadmium red and lemon yellow.

Build up a collection of shade cards and study the effects created when each shade is mixed and allowed to flow in water tracks.

Pigment friends and enemies

Some pigments are transparent and will flow more easily than others, such as alizarin crimson. Others are opaque and will tend to be slower in their action, for example cadmium yellow. I think of them as people and imagine they all have characters. The transparent shades are friendly and will go anywhere with anyone – they will do whatever you wish. The opaques are more bossy and will try to push everyone else out of the way. They will try to tell *you* what to do, dictating how they want to be used. Shades that granulate, like French ultramarine, will form patterns as the small particles of pigment settle in pockets of paper while they dry. These are therefore my decorative friends, such as the poppy in the background on this page.

There is a general belief that watercolour is difficult to control. I suggest that, instead of trying to control it, you should enjoy its many facets and use them to your best advantage. Work with them and become 'best friends' with the medium. It is very easy to fall completely in love with watercolour, and I hope this book will show you why.

Colour mixing

This is an area that I enjoy very much. Not a day goes by when I don't discover a new shade that will be perfect for a given subject. Time spent mixing colour is extremely valuable because not only does it help us learn more about how to achieve perfect shades for each subject, it also helps us learn how individual pigments work.

Mixing secondary colour

Use the same primary colours as on the previous page. Work on a fresh piece of paper and start by mixing equal amounts of alizarin crimson and cobalt blue. You should achieve a vibrant purple. You can mix this colour in the palette or directly on the paper. Add a fresh clean track of water alongside the circle of pigment as in the first exercise and watch the colour flow. By observing the flow and speed of movement of the colour you will learn how much time you have to work on a large painting before the colour dries.

Example of mixing colour on paper. Look at the exciting patterns forming as the colours mix together.

Almost Hare
46 x 61cm (18 x 24in)
The colours in this painting were allowed to mix on the paper and not mixed in the palette.

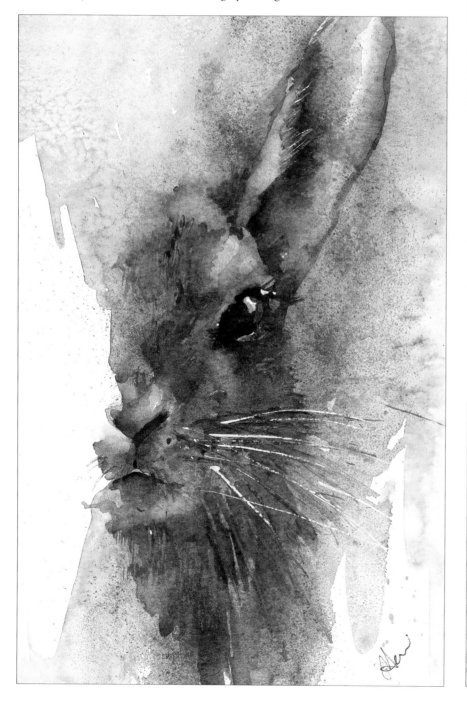

Tip

Practise and experiment with colour. Try new shades. Experiment with contrasts and harmony. Learn about pigments, how they react with other shades, how easily they flow with water and how they dry. This will make you a far better artist than someone who works directly from the tube or pan with no colour mixing and no knowledge of how the pigments work together. Be a better artist!

Repeat the exercise mixing equal parts cadmium yellow and alizarin crimson to achieve a brilliant shade of orange. Finally, add an equal mix of cobalt blue and cadmium yellow to achieve a versatile green. Bear in mind that you can obtain many more wonderful results simply by adjusting the amount of each colour you mix from the primary selection. You can also achieve many more shades by using three different primary colours: try cadmium red, French ultramarine and lemon yellow.

Don't be afraid to experiment – it can lead to wonderful colour mixes, which in turn can produce beautiful results in your paintings. Avoid using colour straight from a tube or pan and you will discover an exciting world of magical shades that make your paintings unique. Always be original in your work.

Colour selection

The value of taking time to experiment with colour mixing is evident in the beauty of paintings that capture a subject perfectly. The more accurate the colour choice, the more realistic a subject will be. Time taken on colour choices should never be rushed; see them as an exciting challenge, and fascinating to create.

Never attempt to start a painting until you know which colours you will use throughout the piece. It is a surprisingly common mistake amongst artists to get virtually to the end of a painting and then get stuck on a final colour choice, for example the background. Know exactly before you pick up your brush which colours you will be using and where. It is the time taken *before* we paint that makes our results successful.

Understanding the formulation of each pigment will help you create incredible work. Choosing a translucent colour like alizarin crimson and using it heavily diluted will give you a wonderful colour choice for a tomato. When combined with an opaque cadmium like cadmium red you have the winning combination of a bossy friend pushing a kind one out of the way, which gives a wonderful interplay of personalities on paper. Get to know your watercolour friends and how they interact.

Try this

For a real challenge find a variety of subjects, for example a still-life object, a piece of fruit and a green leaf, and take time creating exact colours to match them. Study them closely and decide which primary colours would work best as a base for mixing a good match. Keep shade charts of all of your mixes as a permanent record of how you created them. I discovered beautiful skin tones purely by experimenting with alizarin crimson and yellow ochre, for example.

Harmony and contrast

Once you have chosen the right shade for your subject think about what colours would work best in the background. What shades complement the subject, or add impact or drama? Create harmony for quieter paintings and bold contrasts for stronger images that demand this kind of attention. Study your subject in different light for guidance on which colours to select.

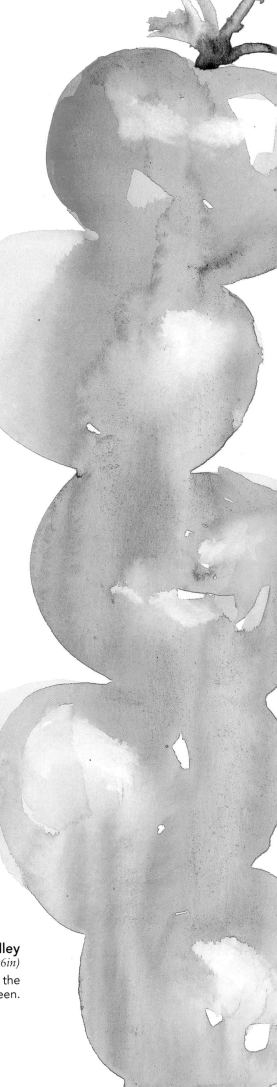

Tomato Medley
20.5 x 41cm (8 x 16in)
An example of translucent shades giving the
illusion of light and sheen.

Light and how we see it

Light or intrigue?

I have often considered that I may see things completely differently from a non-artist. A friend can see sunlight, whereas I see how the sun's rays affect everything they touch, creating complex patterns that can change a simple subject into a vision of intrigue. I strongly believe this is the key factor in creating an excellent painting.
A touch of mystery will draw the viewer back to a painting for a second or a third glance. The ability to see light and capture it creates magic that takes the boring and ordinary into the realms of incredible and extraordinary.

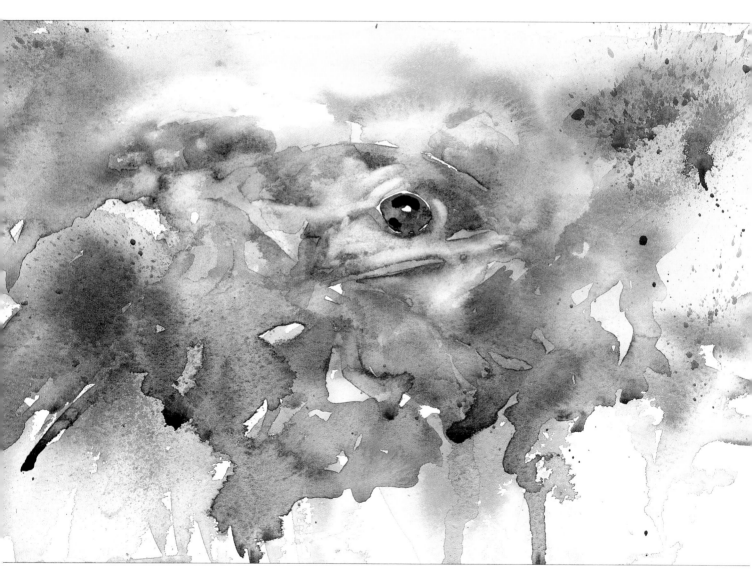

Frog in Autumn Leaves
35.5 x 25.5cm (14 x 10in)
The subject formed out of a first wash of exciting colour. The attraction of this subject was the brilliant sunlight hitting the frog's head.

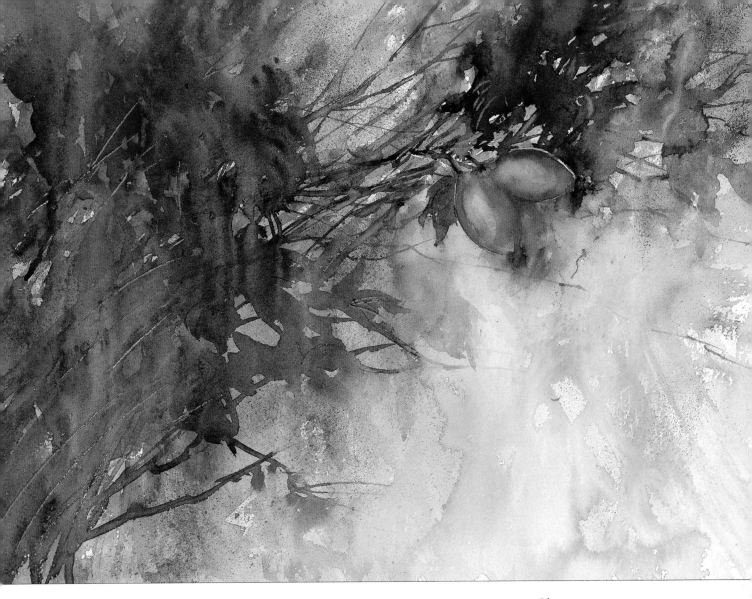

Autumn Glory
71 x 66cm (28 x 26in)

A combination of directional
brushstrokes and vibrant use of
colour gives the viewer an illusion of
light hitting the subject.

Throughout the day, light can make the same scene appear completely
different; sometimes forming a halo or a silhouette, and at other times making
shadow patterns from a subject's form. It is absolutely fascinating. Every way
I turn I see new possibilities for paintings, each with a unique set of qualities
that brings it to life.

Thinking as an artist

The main aim when we pick up our brushes is to create a painting that is
unique and interesting – one that evokes emotion or brings a subject to life.
To achieve this sense of feeling in our paintings we need to see in a way that
excites us. We need to be able to recognise immediately what could make a
great painting, and then know how we can use colour and light to create a
magical interpretation of any given subject.

Simple highlights

By wise choices of colour and clever handling of light, the simplest of subjects
can become the most fascinating. When new artists try to think about what
light means, they often imagine a highlight in an eye or a light section that
brings a small subject to life, as in the painting of rosehips above. Here, light
shining on the round fruits brings a large painting to life, when in fact this is
just a very simple autumn scene. It is the highlight and rich colour that make
this composition work.

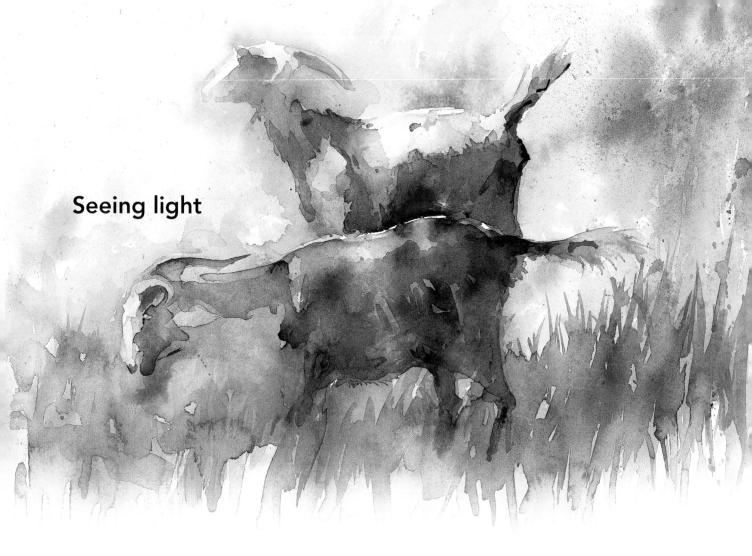

Seeing light

How we see light is what makes us unique as artists. If you look closely at the painting of two goats you will see a subtle line of light on the back of the goat nearest to you. This was the main focal point for me – not the animals. It was the light that attracted me. It immediately caught my attention when I first saw this scene in Turkey. The whole painting evolved around this small area. Where I couldn't see clearly due to the intense sunlight I omitted detail. The head of the goat in the distance is less clear than that of the goat in the foreground. I was guided by my passion for seeing light.

Look at the original scene in the photograph of the two goats grazing. Discover how sections of light make this work as a composition. If we dismiss the light, we are left with a very ordinary scene. Add light, and it instantly becomes far more exciting. Take time to observe the line of light and think about why you think it attracted me. Later in the book I will talk about a technique called 'trapping the light', which is a way of working with scenes such as this one (see page 28).

Just Grazing
51 x 46cm (20 x 18in)

Observe how this painting is created using blocks of colour as opposed to painting a goat literally.

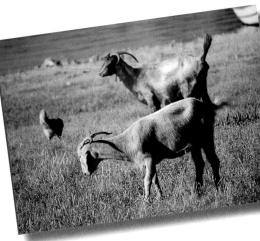

A photograph of goats in Turkey. Study the patterns created by light.

Light illusions

By seeing light and learning how to incorporate it in our work, we can create illusions. We can draw the viewer into seeing a sunny day, imagining movement and so on. Look at the painting of a gondolier on the page opposite and try to imagine this was painted with the subject in the shade. It is impossible, isn't it? Now look at the original photograph taken in Venice. By using my imagination and subtle colour changes, I have given the impression of sunshine. It is well worth learning how light can dramatically create more interest in a painting.

So, before we even pick up our brush we need to think about where light plays a part in the composition, and to observe how it impacts on the subject.

22

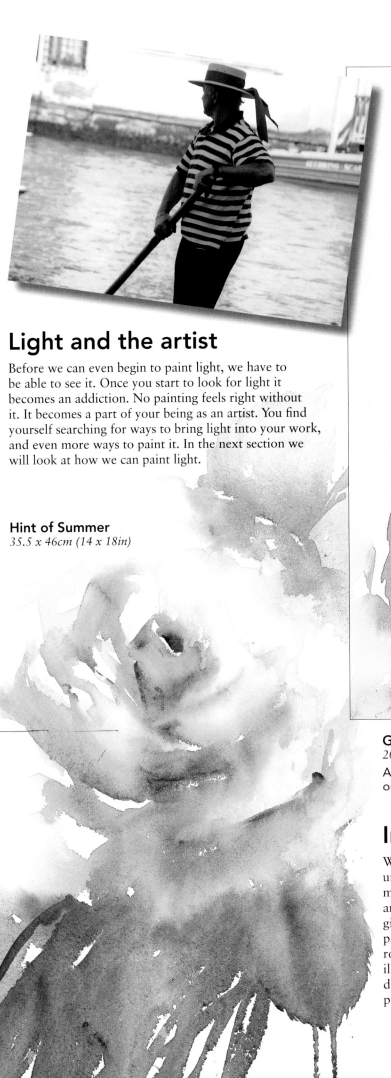

Light and the artist

Before we can even begin to paint light, we have to be able to see it. Once you start to look for light it becomes an addiction. No painting feels right without it. It becomes a part of your being as an artist. You find yourself searching for ways to bring light into your work, and even more ways to paint it. In the next section we will look at how we can paint light.

Hint of Summer
35.5 x 46cm (14 x 18in)

Gondolier Study, with play on light
20.5 x 30.5cm (8 x 12in)
A study changing the source of light from the original photograph taken in Venice.

Imaginative light

We may not always see real light, but once we have understood how it can turn the simple into the magical, we can look at subjects with an artist's eyes and bring them to life more dramatically. We can give the viewer's imagination a part to play in any painting. Is there a feeling of light dancing on these roses, or is it just a trick? Is the artist forming an illusion, disguising what is really there? The missing detail gives the impression that brilliant sunlight is playing with what we can and can't see.

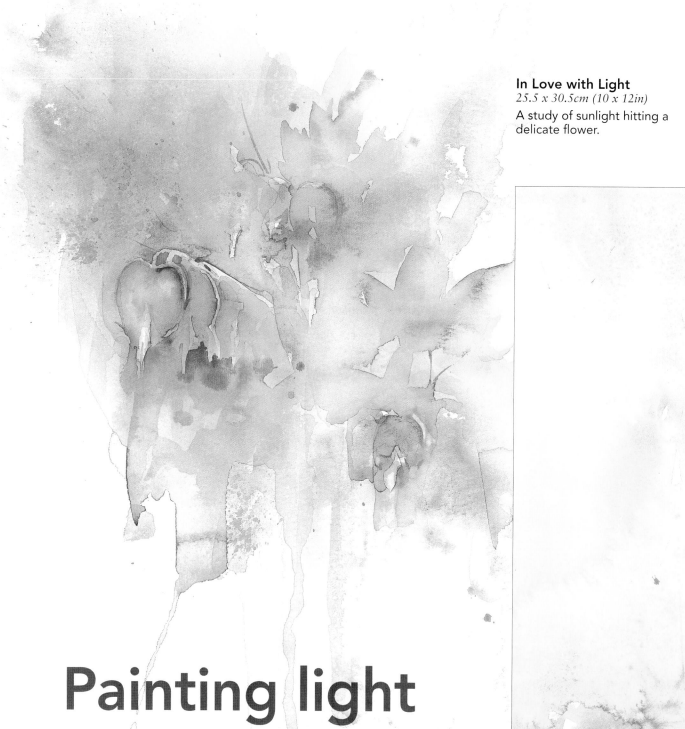

In Love with Light
25.5 x 30.5cm (10 x 12in)
A study of sunlight hitting a delicate flower.

Painting light

If you think seeing light is exciting, try deliberately setting out to paint it! Put the subject completely out of your mind and focus only on where you can see light. It is a fascinating exercise. All of a sudden your whole world becomes a far more interesting place as you observe brilliant colour combinations. You begin to see in a different way, nothing is boring any more, and everything around you becomes potentially far more interesting to paint. Simple things, like the way a shaft of light falls on a single blade of grass, or a single petal on a daisy that is a brilliant white compared with the others because it is in stronger sunshine, become abstract compositions just waiting to be captured on paper. You start looking for highlights and shadows. You notice how the sun's rays affect buildings and architecture. Introducing light into our paintings injects them with a feeling of life, and there are many wonderful ways of doing this.

Choosing colour that portrays light

So, how do you start to paint light? One of the most obvious options is to choose colour that brings an instant feeling of warmth and sunshine into your work. Bright shades can portray light beautifully. Contrasts of cool colour located against warm shades also work well.

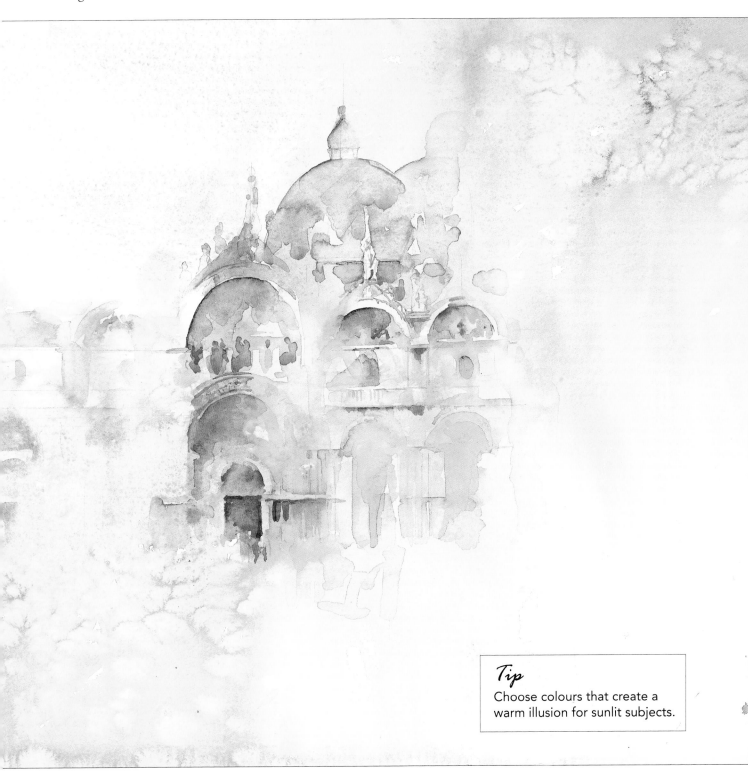

> *Tip*
> Choose colours that create a warm illusion for sunlit subjects.

St Paul's Study, London
56 x 38cm (22 x 15in)

In this study of St Paul's Cathedral in London, a selection of cadmium orange and quinacridone gold gives an illusion of the building being hit by brilliant sunshine. Inconsistent depth of the same colour throughout the study also creates the illusion of sun rays hitting the façade.

Working with small highlights

A favourite technique with many artists is to use small, simple, specifically placed highlights. These give an impression of light reflected by or hitting a given subject. For example, look at the eyes in the study of a mouse. Small sections of white can be a really helpful way to add a sense of life to a painting.

Leaving white sections

Another technique is to leave whole sections of white paper throughout the subject or composition, as in the painting of the herb picker below. Unlike the effect achieved with small highlights, we now have the impression of blinding sunlight.

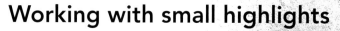

Mouse Study
25.5 x 20.5cm (10 x 8in)
White highlights and hints of the subject bring this small mouse to life.

Tip

Vary the same colour to create illusions of light hitting a subject and to add extra intrigue, mystery and interest.

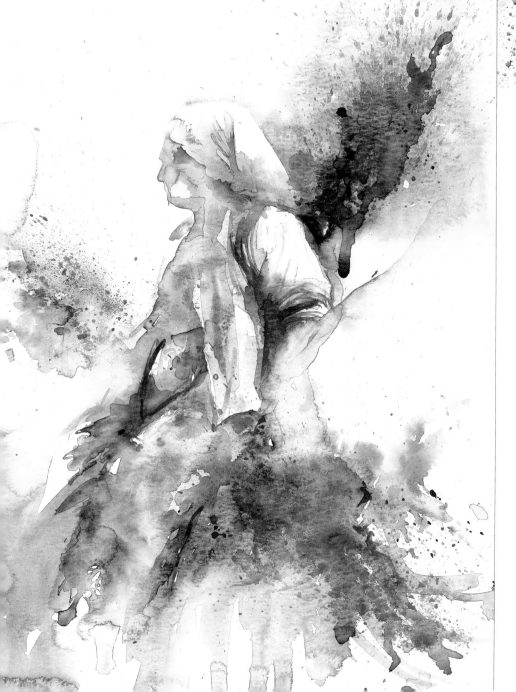

The Herb Picker, Turkey
46 x 56cm (18 x 22in)
Look at the figure resting in brilliant sunshine. If you study the trousers you will notice the red flowers on the material vary in depth of colour. The lighter sections look less vibrant so are possibly not in the direct rays of sunlight.

Using dark contrasts of colour against light

A very common technique for painting light is to use dark colours against a light area to create a strong contrast. This not only gives an illusion of light, it also creates a background that makes the focal point far more dramatic. This is demonstrated well if you look at the dark colour against the lighter section on the main elephant's head in *Almost There*. Here, the flash of turquoise makes a creative impact on the finished painting. It is unexpected and brings excitement to an otherwise uncomplicated mixture of harmonious colours.

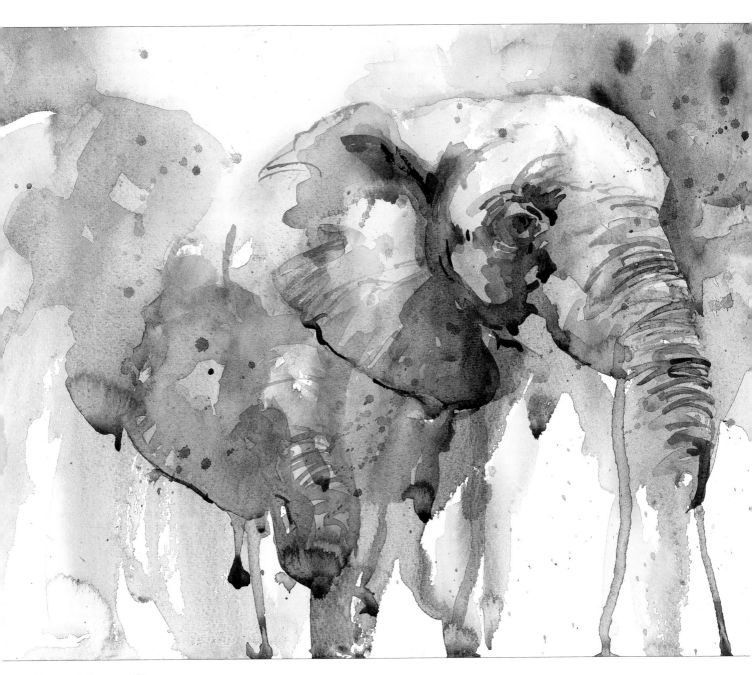

Almost There, Africa
61 x 51cm (24 x 20in)
Leaving sections for the viewer's imagination creates magical interest.

> *Tip*
> Add impact by using unusual colour additions and strong contrasts of bold and soft colour.

Trapping the light

There are times when you can clearly see subjects surrounded by light, almost like a halo effect. Light sections around the hints of figures in the background of *Walking in Murano* opposite creates an illusion of brilliant sunlight. At times you can clearly see a well-defined line of light trapped between two subjects, as in the painting of goats grazing on page 22. This is a wonderful time to use a technique called 'trapping the light' (see below and page 30).

Colour fusions

Losing detail and allowing colours to merge can soften a painting and give a wonderful feeling of movement. See, for example, the painting *Walking in Murano* opposite. It can also create a sense, again, of blinding sunlight. Too many tiny details can be distracting in a painting. Always simplify your work and keep the attention on your main focal point or confuse the viewer with expressive application of colour.

Capturing light combinations

There are many ways to incorporate light in a painting: clever use of colour, leaving sections white, adding highlights, blurring detail with lost and found edges. A combination of all or any of these techniques can result in an incredible painting – one that not only intrigues the viewer but also gives pleasure to the artist whilst the painting is being executed.

   In the next section we will look a little more closely at some of the techniques used, and start pulling together all of the ideas described so far on how to see and paint light.

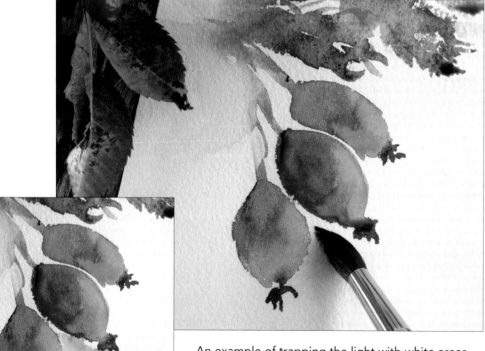

An example of trapping the light with white areas between each subject.

Softening edges can give an illusion of life and movement.

Walking in Murano
61 x 56cm (24 x 22in)
Lost and found edges with fusions of colour create a sense of light hitting both subjects
and their surroundings on a brilliantly sunny day in Murano.

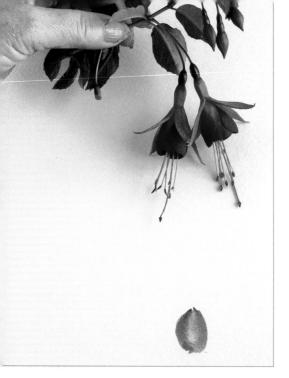

Fuchsia study

If you cannot wait any longer to pick up a paintbrush and try out the ideas you have learnt about so far, here is a simple exercise in painting colour and light minus the use of a preliminary sketch. Try this, then learn about the techniques you can use to help you excel as an artist.

1 Look at the subject closely, then start by placing neat colour on to the paper.

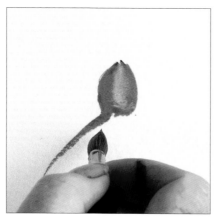

2 Load your brush with clean water and pull out the pink sepals using curved brushstrokes.

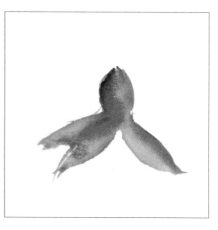

3 Load the brush with neat pigment and drop it into the wash. Allow the colour to blend on the paper, resulting in colour fusions.

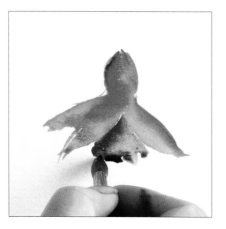

4 Using neat pigment, paint in the purple petals. Take the colour into the red and allow them to fuse on the paper.

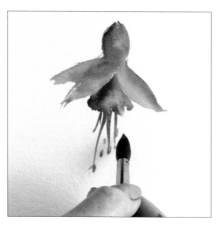

5 With the tip of the brush, pull down some stamens and dot the anthers on the ends.

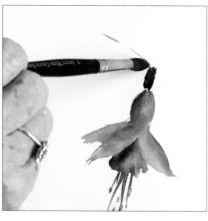

6 Put in the ovary and stalk at the base of the flower.

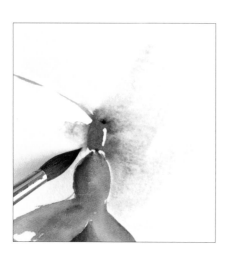

7 Lay on water around the right-hand side of the ovary and bleed out the colour. Dampen the left-hand side also and soften.

8 Leaving a white space around the subject to trap the light adds interest.

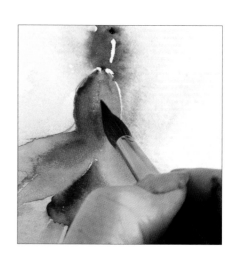

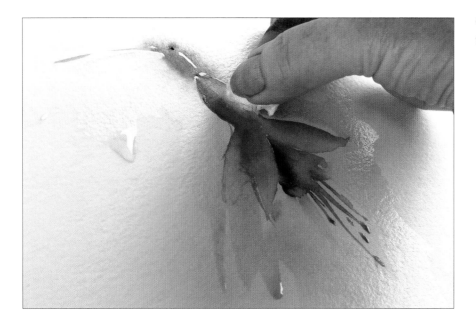

9 If necessary, lift a small highlight with tissue.

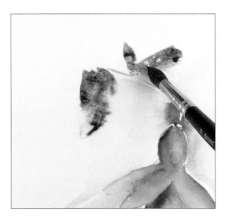

10 Put in the leaves on the stalk.

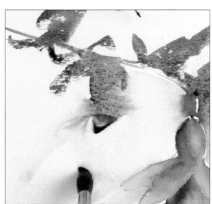

11 Soften edges with clean water for an illusion of movement.

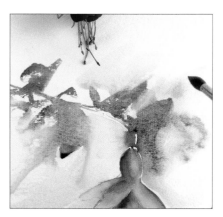

12 Build up the painting gradually.

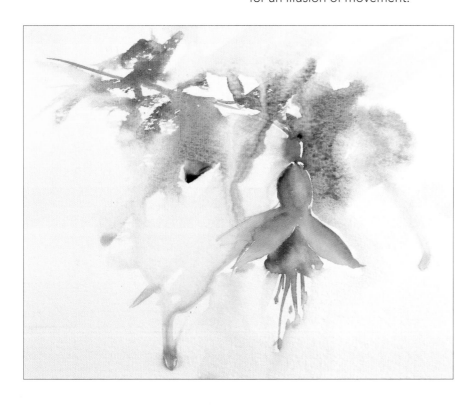

Fuschia Study

Stop when you feel you can see your subject. Do not overwork or worry about adding too much detail.

Techniques

When I first started painting I studied numerous basic techniques. Many I still use, while others I have completely discarded. I have grown as an artist and my style has evolved; over time, I have created my own way of working. What once seemed difficult when I was a beginner has now become easy with practice and, dare I say, what I first learned years ago now seems so boring. It is far easier to explain what I mean by looking at my favourite techniques in watercolour and how I have adapted them to make my own work original, more exciting and unique.

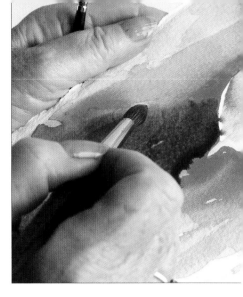

Bleeding colour away from a negative space.

Washes

Every artist needs to start at the beginning, so working with basic washes is a wonderful way to learn how to work with this magical medium. Washes allow pigment to flow and cover paper in a variety of ways. A simple wash can make a beautiful backdrop for a sky, whilst placing a complex wash in the foreground can really add impact to the most peaceful of scenes.

Rural Study
61 x 56cm (24 x 22in)
Basic washes with a touch of excitement as 'old' meet 'new' techniques in a landscape.

Daffodil: the first wash. Glorious
colour forms a hint of the subject as
a base for a painting.

A flat wash in one even colour, a graded wash working from darker to light
sections on paper, or a varied wash with a combination of shades can create
mood and interest. Choosing the right colour and brushstrokes for an initial
wash can make a dramatic difference, giving amazing results that can seem far
more alive and vibrant. Dare to be different! Take time to think about your
first wash as it will be the most important foundation for a successful painting.

In my paintings, initial washes come strongly into play to create unusual
formations of colour throughout the composition. I work minus a preliminary
sketch, placing colour directly in position to form the foundation of my
finished piece. I then work in layers, building up detail in sections via use of
creative brushwork and watercolour techniques.

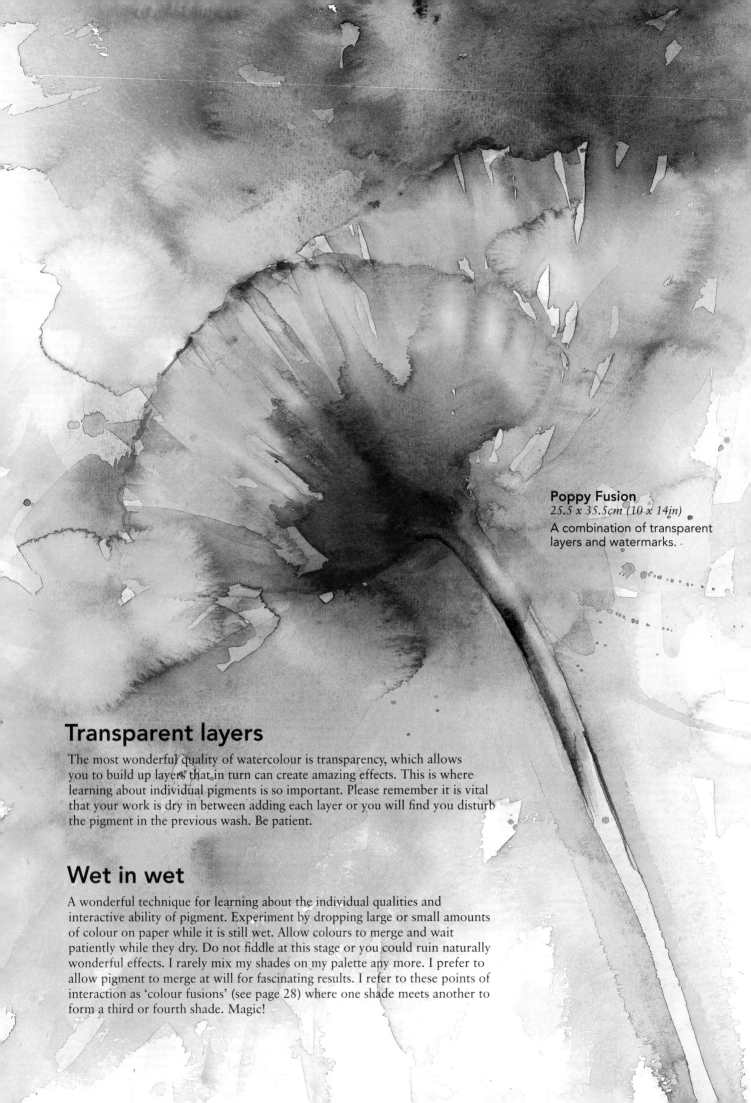

Poppy Fusion
25.5 x 35.5cm (10 x 14in)
A combination of transparent layers and watermarks.

Transparent layers

The most wonderful quality of watercolour is transparency, which allows you to build up layers that in turn can create amazing effects. This is where learning about individual pigments is so important. Please remember it is vital that your work is dry in between adding each layer or you will find you disturb the pigment in the previous wash. Be patient.

Wet in wet

A wonderful technique for learning about the individual qualities and interactive ability of pigment. Experiment by dropping large or small amounts of colour on paper while it is still wet. Allow colours to merge and wait patiently while they dry. Do not fiddle at this stage or you could ruin naturally wonderful effects. I rarely mix my shades on my palette any more. I prefer to allow pigment to merge at will for fascinating results. I refer to these points of interaction as 'colour fusions' (see page 28) where one shade meets another to form a third or fourth shade. Magic!

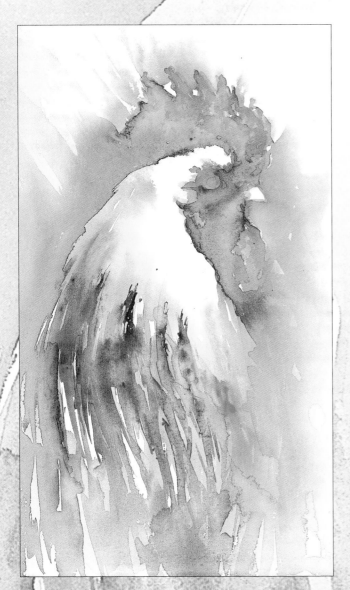

Watermarks and runs

I couldn't help but smile when I wrote this section. After years of studying how to create the perfect flat wash minus any hints of watermarks or runs, I now find myself praying for them to occur! It is the imperfections that prove a watercolour is genuine. No other medium has the ability to react on paper in the way watercolour does so I now celebrate its magical qualities and allow each watermark to shine in a painting. I aim to create them and feel that buzz of excitement when I see a brilliant 'happy accident' whilst eagerly incorporating it into my work.

Tip

Work with your paper at an angle to create intricate patterns in your work!

Cockerel Study
20.5 x 30.5cm (8 x 12in)

Creative first wash of a cockerel using a mixed wash of wet in wet, directional brushstrokes and colour fusions. Colour fusions occur where pigment has been allowed to merge on wet paper and form patterns. These are encouraged by a subtle dropping action from the brush in a carefully aimed and directional movement of the arm.

Flow of Anemone
30.5 x 35.5cm (12 x 14in)

Allowing water to flow creates patterns within this vase of anemones. A magical fusion of colour that is almost impossible to repeat, which makes this result quite unique. A 'run', where colour flows down the paper, adds drama and a feeling of movement. Runs also form a sense of connection between sections and colour. To me, they are an indication of what watercolour can do, and are a trademark of many of my paintings.

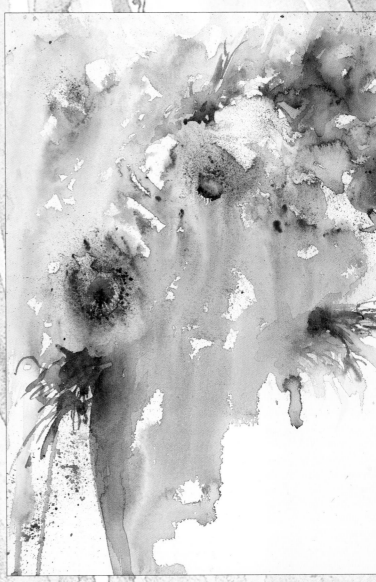

Texture by splattering

Simply by splattering colour with a toothbrush you can soften a boring area of a painting and bring it to life. But why stop with the toothbrush? Why not try splattering colour directly from a loaded brush in directional aims at the paper? Even more exciting, while the colour on your paper is still wet, load a brush with clean water and throw that at the paper. Allow it to push pigment out of the way to form amazing fusions of colour and light sections. Have fun experimenting and don't settle for anything other than terrific results in your work.

Lifting

This is a technique I will mention with caution. Lifting with a gentle use of the brush to remove a small amount of colour is a technique that can be used to give the effect of light hitting a subject or simply to add interest. Take care, though, because this technique can also easily kill a painting. Why? The surface of any watercolour paper will only tolerate so much handling. If you are too aggressive you can ruin both the surface and your chances of obtaining a clean result. So please use this technique wisely.

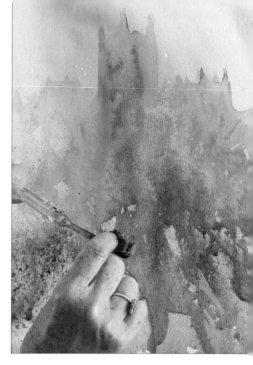

Directional splattering of pigment using an old toothbrush.

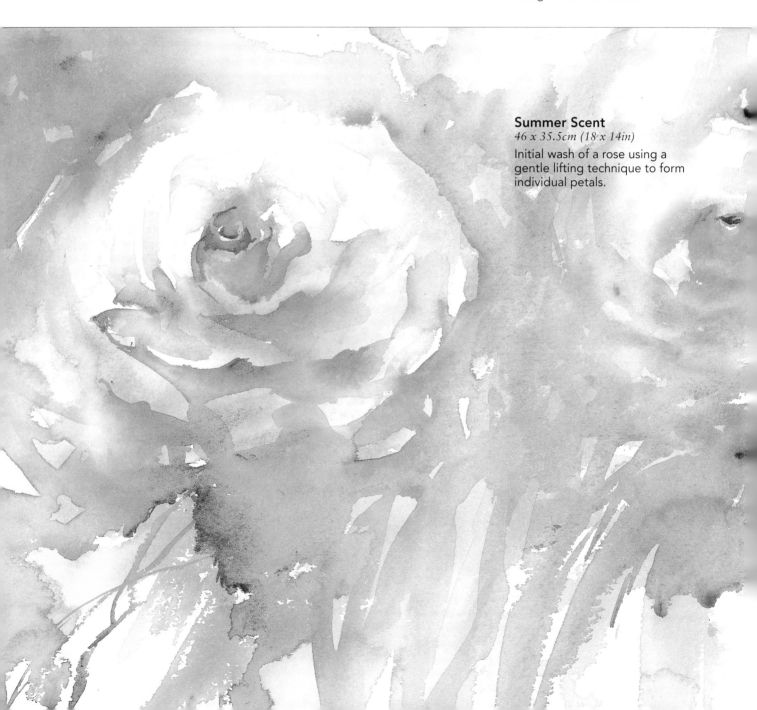

Summer Scent
46 x 35.5cm (18 x 14in)
Initial wash of a rose using a gentle lifting technique to form individual petals.

Directional, varied and interesting brushstrokes

Think about the way you handle a brush. Use soft, gentle strokes for soft subjects
such as fur. Use curved strokes for curved subjects. Think about how many ways you
can use your brush, and make each brushstroke count, no matter how small it is.

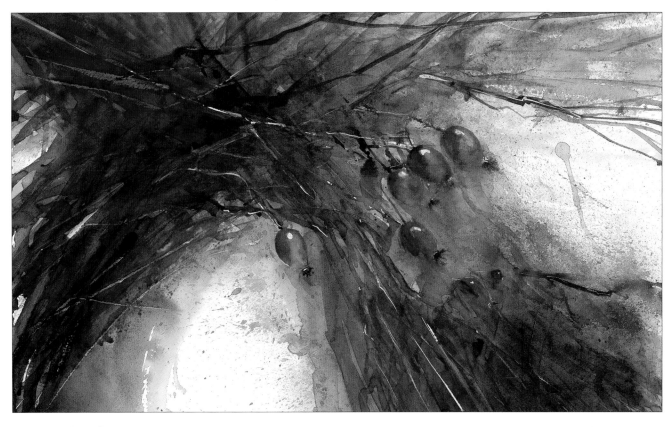

Autumn Jewels
71 x 56cm (28 x 22in)
Colour selection and directional brushstrokes give a feeling of drama to an otherwise simple
scene of twigs and rosehips.

Negative painting

Simply by painting around a negative space can give a wonderful effect to
many subects, as in the painting *Honesty Seed Heads* opposite.

Salt

I am amazed at how many students seem literally to throw salt on a wash and
then expect to achieve miraculous results, when with a little pre-planning
along with controlled application you can create such brilliant effects, and
place them exactly where you want them. Think about where you place the
salt, which direction you apply it and how much you use. I have used salt in
the *Sunflower Explosion* on pages 14–15.

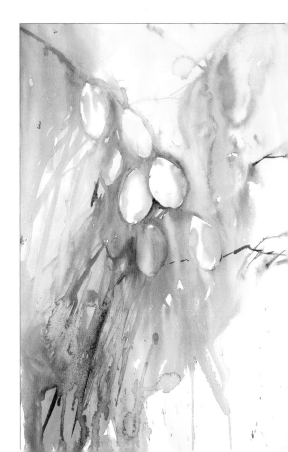

Honesty Seed Heads
56 x 61cm (22 x 24in)
Starting with a varied wash using the negative painting
technique, layers of colour were built up gradually and
directional brushstrokes used. Final detail was then
added to complete the composition.

Composition

This is a wonderful area to look into in detail. There are so many books and studies on this subject alone that could easily confuse the most intelligent of us. What is clear, however, is that an interesting composition can make the difference between a poor painting and one that really works.

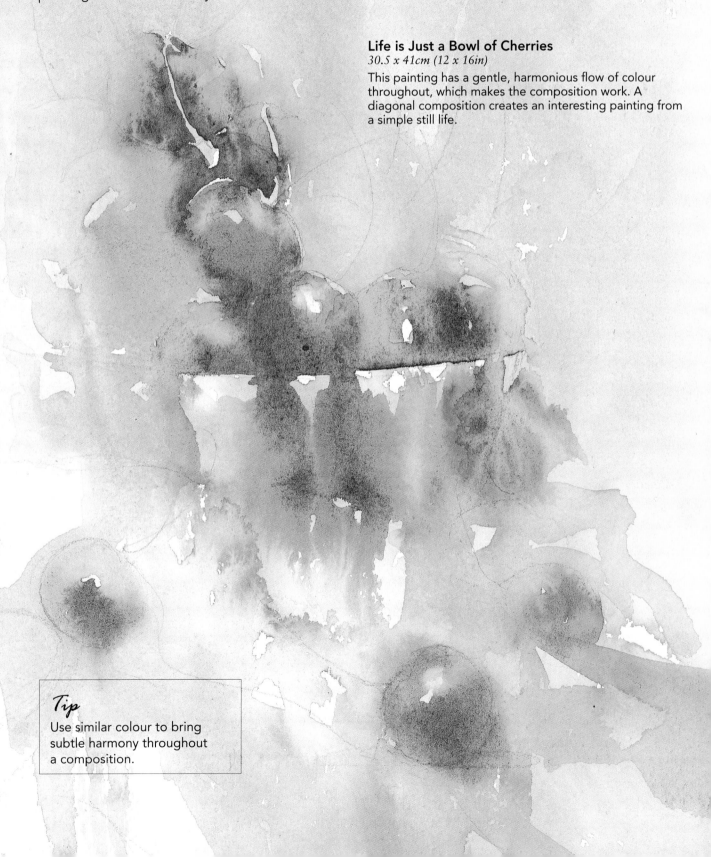

Life is Just a Bowl of Cherries
30.5 x 41cm (12 x 16in)
This painting has a gentle, harmonious flow of colour throughout, which makes the composition work. A diagonal composition creates an interesting painting from a simple still life.

Tip
Use similar colour to bring subtle harmony throughout a composition.

There is a fine line between following basic guidelines and becoming too predictable. If all artists followed every basic rule on how to create a good composition, our paintings could become similar and almost routine. I like my work to be unique and unusual so I often deliberately break rules on how one should paint. I often choose my favourite part of the subject and then work out how I can make that the sole point of the whole composition. Look at *Teilo*.

Some artists avoid placing a subject in the centre of the paper, or even on a central horizon line. However, with simple tricks and knowledge of how to make a composition work, any subject can be placed anywhere on the paper. It is important to think before you pick up the brush as to how to make each painting successful.

With clever understanding of basic principles, there are ways around every 'golden rule'. Have fun, dare to be different and always aim to create a painting that is unique, well thought-out beforehand and exciting.

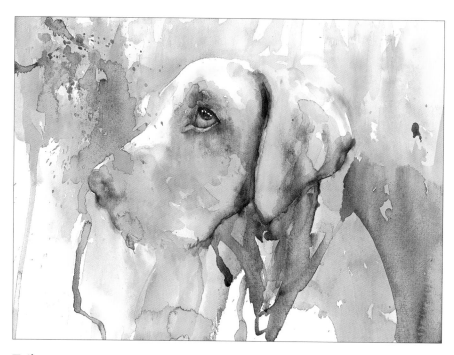

Teilo
66 x 61cm (26 x 24in)

The eye and expression of this gorgeous dog were so beautiful, I made them my focal point. The dog's head is not as you would expect. I worked with colour around this section to make him jump off the paper in an unusual way. The flash of turquoise under his chin makes this really unique and shows off a terrific contrast between the golden shades elsewhere.

Glorious Giant
71 x 61cm (28 x 24in)

This painting of elephants has the subject in the centre of the composition. Energetic brushstrokes accentuate movement, with bold colour contrasts in the right locations adding interest to this exciting scene.

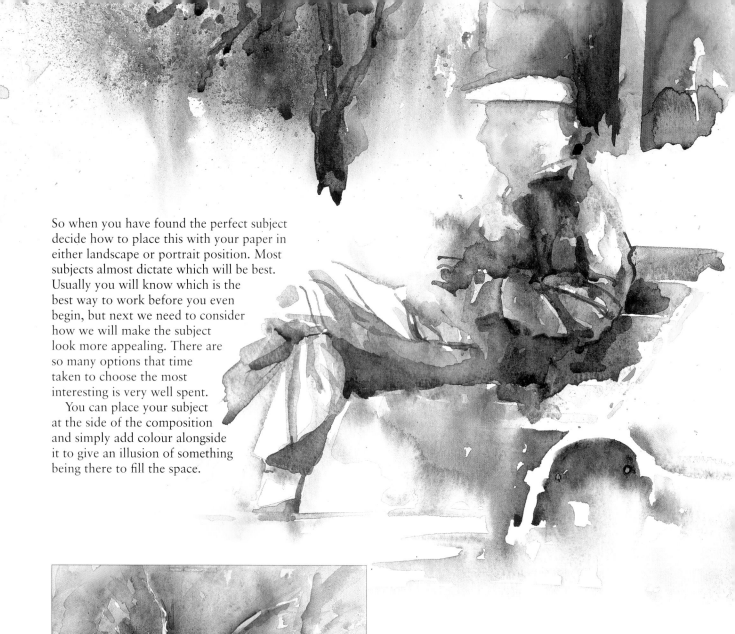

So when you have found the perfect subject decide how to place this with your paper in either landscape or portrait position. Most subjects almost dictate which will be best. Usually you will know which is the best way to work before you even begin, but next we need to consider how we will make the subject look more appealing. There are so many options that time taken to choose the most interesting is very well spent.

You can place your subject at the side of the composition and simply add colour alongside it to give an illusion of something being there to fill the space.

Watching the World Go By
41 x 30.5cm (16 x 12in)
Painted around the play of sunlight, this scene is created with the paper best suited to a horizontal position or landscape.

Tip
Use directional brushstrokes, colour and texture to draw the viewer's eye directly to the main focal point in a composition.

Pigging Out
35.5 x 46cm (14 x 18in)
The main subject is in the upper corner of the composition, with colour placement making this idea work successfully. This worked best in portrait format.

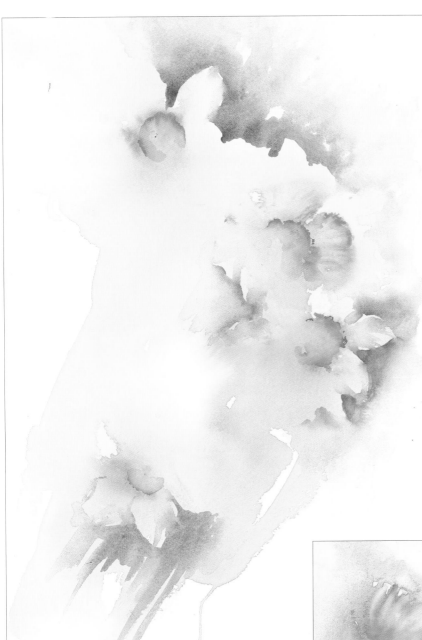

Once you have decided what to paint, spend time thinking about ways to make it different and more alive, and always look for the light in every scene you paint. Think before you pick up the brush. Don't race to begin painting. Consider exactly what will be the background and the foreground, and decide on the harmonious colours throughout well before you start. Even deciding about the angles of your brushstrokes will help you produce a successful composition.

Tip
Look at as many compositions by famous artists as you can and try to work out why they work or why they don't appeal to you.

Essence of Spring
51 x 66cm (20 x 26in)

Be imaginative and look at a variety of ways to place your subject that could be unusual and striking. These daffodils show how a curved or circular placement can often create an effective arrangement.

Poppies of Gold
46 x 56cm (18 x 22in)

We can choose to cover the whole paper with colour, with a sense of movement created purely by directional brushstrokes. The focal point in the poppy painting is the main flower in the upper section of the paper, with everything else painted in less detail to draw the viewer's eye to that point. In fact the background is merely there to showcase the focal point.

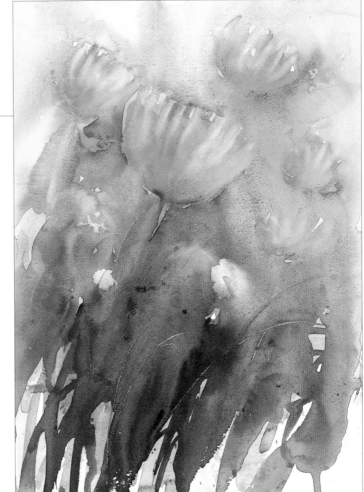

Demonstrations

Are you desperate to paint after all this reading? So am I, so let's race into the step-by-step demonstrations and see how to pull all these ideas into a finished painting.

We have studied colour, light, techniques and composition. Now it is time to see how they all come into play in a painting, but please make sure you fully understand all the previous suggestions before you pick up your brush in order to gain the maximum enjoyment out of each demonstration. And just one more tip: try smiling while you work, you would not believe the difference it makes to your results! A bored artist produces boring paintings and we are aiming for results that positively glow with light, seem to have a sense of movement and life in them and are all absolutely unique!

Before you begin painting, lay out the colours you need around the edge of your palette. Select your mixes and try them out on a piece of scrap paper. Try to visualise the finished painting before you start, and decide where the focal point will be; all of the brushstrokes and colour work will flow towards that point. Preparation is the key to a successful painting.

Beauty of Venice
71 x 66cm (28 x 26in)

This is where being an artist is so brilliant. Using a mixture of all the techniques on pages 32–37 can give a painting that added spark, pulling the viewer back time and time again. Consider working with lost and found edges; add fine detail against loose sections for stunning contrasts. Confuse anyone looking at your work so that they need to use their own imagination to fill in spaces you have deliberately chosen to leave out. But most of all, highlight the light in each painting and use clever colour combinations to make it more important in the piece.

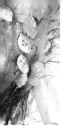

Honesty

This simple project, whose subject is honesty seed heads, otherwise known as the silver dollar plant, begins with painting around negative shapes. You will learn how to allow colours to flow and interact, leave sections affected by light, use colour contrasts to add impact, and eventually produce a soft result in watercolour. Begin by choosing the colours you wish to use.

You will need

300gsm (140lb) rough watercolour paper, approximately 38 x 56cm (15 x 22in)

Paintbrushes: size 8 squirrel pointed wash brush, and size 3 (fine rigger) and size 10 Kolinsky sable watercolour brushes

Painting knife

Toothbrush

Palette

Watercolour paints: perylene maroon, French ultramarine, quinacridone gold, cadmium orange, alizarin crimson, Winsor violet, burnt umber

Designer's white gouache

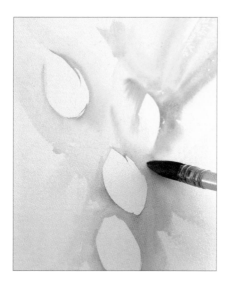

1 Begin with the wash brush. Dampen the brush and load it with dilute alizarin crimson. Paint around the three main seed heads. This area of the paper will remain dry. Before the pigment dries, soften the edges with water and pull away in different directions – this will create water tracks for the colour to run into. Bring some cadmium orange into the water tracks towards the top of the painting to represent sunlight. Create colour fusions by allowing the colours to mix on the paper.

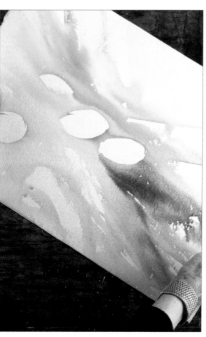

2 Bring in some cooler colours – purple and blue – in the bottom left of the painting and define the edges of the seed heads. Don't be afraid to introduce some intense colour – Winsor violet to the lower corner will bring a feeling of depth to the shadows here, and work with quinacridone gold in the opposite corner (top right) for a wonderful contrast of vibrant shades. All the shades will merge and interact as the painting develops.

Tip
Change the angle of the paper to control the direction in which the paint runs.

3 Continue to intensify the colours. Use alizarin crimson to bring in the twigs in the top right part of the picture. This red will interact with the damp colours already on the paper.

Tip
Colours will always dry paler, so they can be quite strong initially.

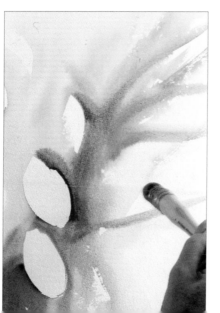

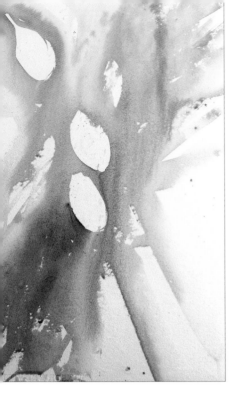

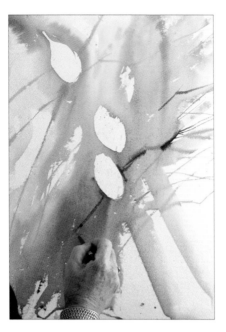

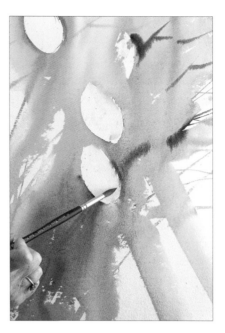

4 Allow the alizarin crimson to flow downwards to the right. Add some splatters of colour using the size 10 brush – red top right and cadmium orange bottom left. Turn the paper to force the paint to run and create glorious colour fusions. The first wash is now complete and you are ready to move on to the next layer.

5 Using the smallest brush, start to add the fine twigs. Use burnt umber. Try to obtain a sense of flow through the painting. Stop every now and then to allow the colours to fuse.

6 With the size 10 brush, bleed the background colour into each of the seed heads. Do this by wetting the inside of the seed head with a damp brush, and just touching the edge of the shape with the brush so that the colour runs into it. Allow the colour fusions to develop before continuing with the painting.

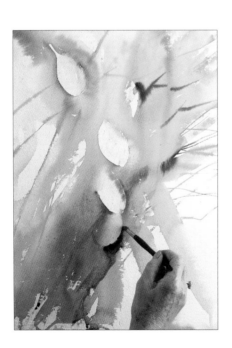

7 Use your imagination to develop the painting and build up the layers. Bring in some cadmium orange to define the edges of the main seed heads, and to outline more seed head 'ghosts' in the background. Lay on more red and purple, allowing colours to run and blend into each other.

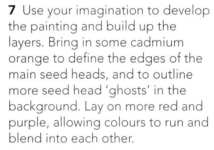

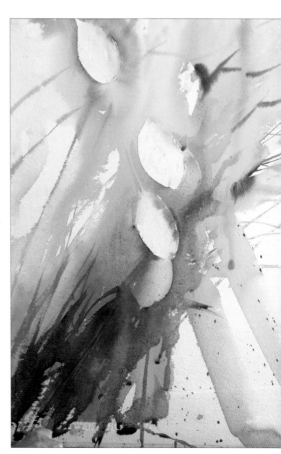

Tip

Try to gain a sense of freedom as you work – bring in light where you want light, and dark where you want dark.

8 Flick your painting with water and splatter with colour, building up the painting to create diagonal movement across the paper. Work carefully around the main focal point so as not to detract from it. Bring in more colour to define the 'ghosts' and to accentuate the dark area in the lower left-hand corner. Add more stems to this area of the painting – draw some into the paint using the tip of the painting knife.

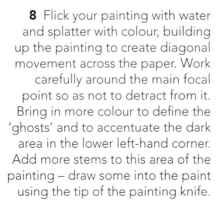

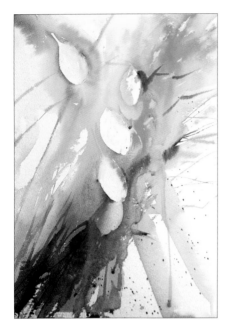

9 Move to the top right of the painting and bring in strong orange colours to accentuate the light area. Continue to define the seed heads, softening the edges as you work. Splatter the lower right of the painting with purple and the lower left with plain water to create bursts of colour.

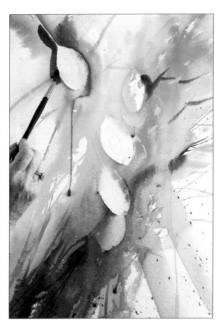

10 Focusing now on the top left, put a wash of purple over the red. Here you are aiming to strengthen colour in a few sections of the painting. Paint carefully around the seed heads and gently bleed the purple away.

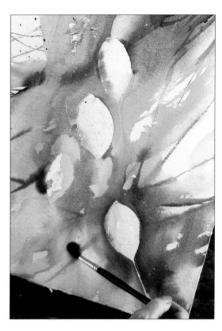

11 Introduce some French ultramarine into the top left corner, and use it to define more 'ghosts'. Turn the painting upside down to bleed out the colour. Bring more purple into the top of the painting to create harmony. Keep moving and adding drama to each section.

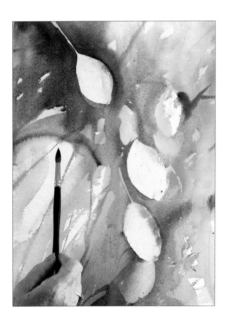

12 Turn the painting back up the right way and introduce an arch of blue on the left. Hold the brush at the end and use your whole arm to bring in more twigs.

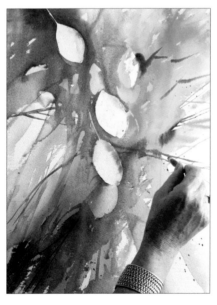

13 Continue to build up the painting – by now, it should be painting itself! Add more twigs where needed, and lay washes inside the seed heads as before. Stand back and observe your painting before continuing with the next layer.

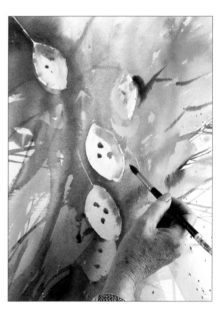

14 Start to build up the colour within the seed heads – just a little, to give them form and depth. Bring in some dots of burnt umber mixed with a little orange to represent the seeds. Circle each seed with water to trap the light (see page 28).

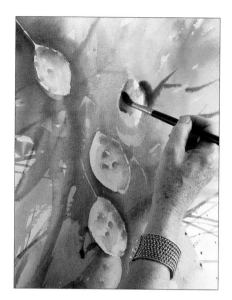

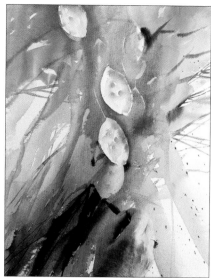

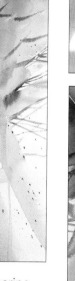

Tip

As a general rule, make each corner of your painting different.

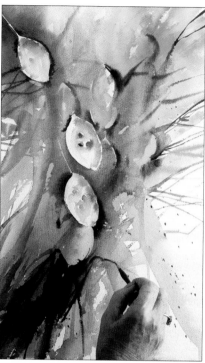

15 Soften the seed heads and use the tip of the brush to create a circle of light around each seed. Accentuate the background 'ghosts' where necessary. Reassess your painting and decide which areas need further definition. All the elements of the painting are now in place – you now need to start to pulling it together. Only work on the areas you are not happy with – leave those you like alone.

16 Mix some French ultramarine and burnt umber and introduce some dark twigs, starting in the lower left corner. Carefully go round the edges of the seed heads and soften the background where necessary. Add a few connecting strokes to draw the painting together and create harmony.

17 Bring in some more twigs bottom left using red, and define the seeds within the main seed head using maroon (but avoid overworking). Change to the size 3 brush and, using dry brushwork, introduce contrast by adding dark, thin lines here and there. Place fine lines around parts of the seed heads to define their base.

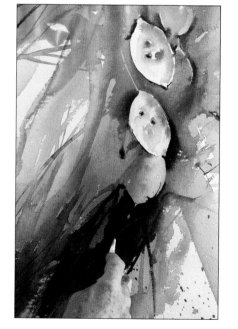

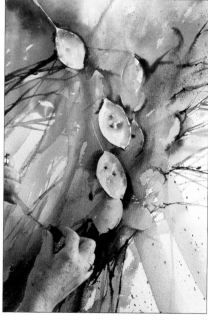

19 Further define some of the darker twigs using red and purple, then splatter into the painting using the toothbrush. Think carefully about where the paint is going, and avoid splattering in one direction only. Use red and purple over the orange areas, red on the purple, and dark purple on the light purple for contrast.

18 Scrape out some light twigs in the bottom right of the picture using the tip of the painting knife, then reassess your painting.

Tip

If you place a light colour behind a stronger version of the same one, the light colour will appear further away in the distance.

47

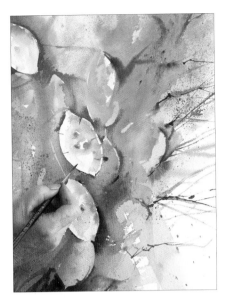

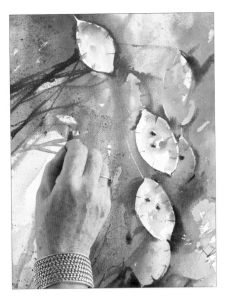

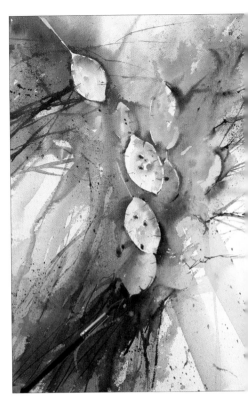

20 Using the smallest brush and purple paint, place six tiny lines around the inner edges of the main seed heads. Add a few to the 'ghosts' as well – not too many; just enough to show what they are.

21 Strengthen the colours within the two main seed heads, avoiding overworking, and add some more thin lines here and there to make the painting more realistic and bring it to life.

Tip
Avoid repetition and boring results!

22 For more life and movement, use the larger brush to add directional splatters – purple top right and orange lower left – until you are happy with the result. Leave the painting to dry before moving on to the final stage.

Tip
Be careful not to add too much gouache – the best results are obtained when the highlights are subtle and delicately placed.

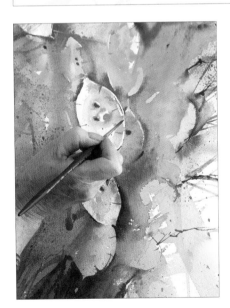

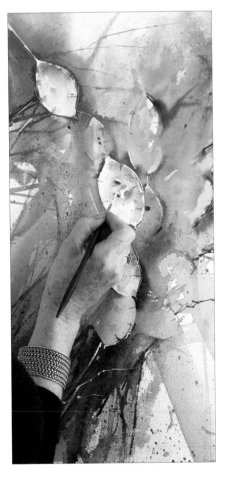

23 Once the painting is dry, add a touch of gouache (it's important not to add too much). Use the size 3 brush and add it here and there to give a feeling of movement and depth to the picture and inject it with life. Use it also to correct the shapes of the main elements if necessary, but avoid following all the lines too closely.

24 Bring a little light into the centre of the main seed head by placing tiny highlights on some of the seeds. Finally add a few directional lines to mimic twigs that are in bright sunlight.

Honesty Seed Heads
38 x 56cm (15 x 22in)
A fusion of vibrant colour of varying intensity, along with directional brushstrokes, add impact and drama to a very simple subject.

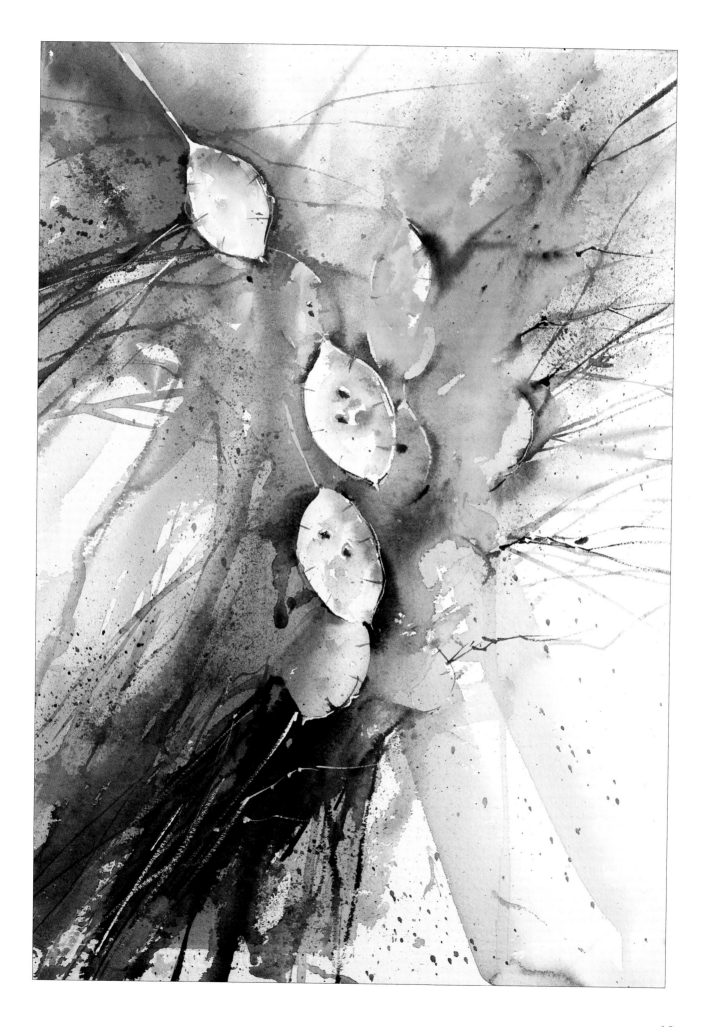

Celebration of Colour

Once you have mastered the basic foundation in this simple landscape, you can work on further scenes making them as complex or as simple as you wish. Choose colours to portray the mood, atmosphere and season in either an abstract or more realistic style.

As before, begin by laying out the colours in your palette, and try out your mixes on a scrap piece of paper before placing them on your painting.

You will need

300gsm (140lb) rough watercolour paper, 56 x 38cm (22 x 15in)

Paintbrushes: size 8 squirrel pointed wash brush, and size 3 (fine rigger) and size 10 Kolinsky sable watercolour brushes

Painting knife

Palette

Ruler or card

Toothbrush

Salt

Watercolour paints: perylene maroon, quinacridone gold, cadmium orange, alizarin crimson, Winsor violet, cobalt turquoise

Designer's white gouache

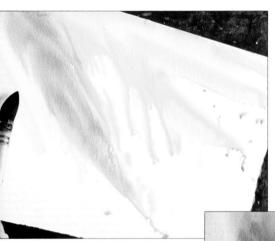

1 Working with the paper at an angle, use the wash brush. Begin by laying in tracks of clean water across the paper flowing top left to bottom right. Create runs using diluted orange pigment. Keep the lower left of the painting 'quiet', as used in a 'whisper' of colour (see page 17).

2 Splatter in some alizarin crimson and tilt the paper to create bold runs.

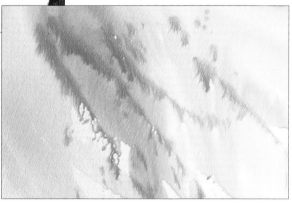

3 Change to the size 10 brush and splatter in some orange, turquoise and perylene maroon at the bottom of the picture. Turn the paper upside down to direct the colour up towards the top of the painting. The aim is to gain a sense of darker colours in the foreground and lighter colours in the background.

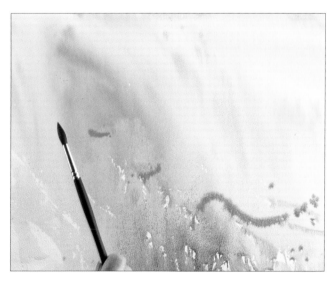

4 Lay clean water over the lower left part of the painting to allow colour to blend into it. Splatter in more orange over the bottom half. Enjoy the effect of the pigment as it fuses with the water. You are aiming to create a combination of colours with interesting water effects.

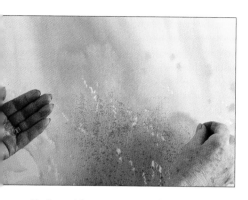

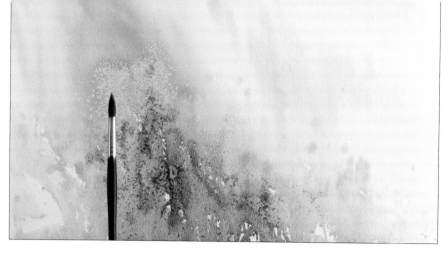

5 Sprinkle on some salt, aiming it directionally from the bottom to the top of the painting. This technique adds texture to the foreground.

6 Continue to splatter on colour to build up the initial wash and create atmosphere. Use gold, a little purple, and lastly turquoise, violet and red in varying amounts. Allow the colour fusions to develop and leave to dry. At this point, you can add more layers of paint and salt to build up the colour and texture if you wish.

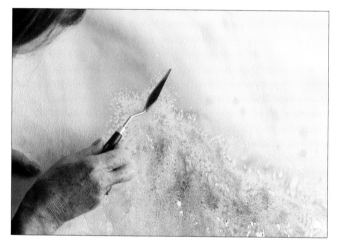

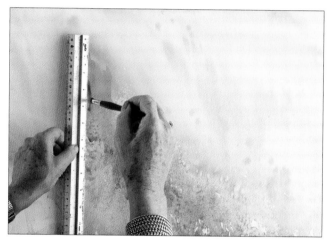

7 When dry, gently scrape off the salt using the edge of the painting knife. The salt disperses the pigment, and so leaves a pattern once it is removed. You are now ready to start work on the buildings.

8 Place a ruler or card vertically where you wish the left-hand side of the castle to be placed. Paint a broad orange stroke down the ruler. Bleed the colour away, taking it down and across the painting, then add in some red. Allow the paint to run down the painting – these runs will add pattern, texture and colour to the foreground. Both are translucent colours, so the pattern formed by the salt will still be visible underneath.

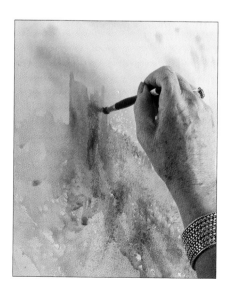

9 Very carefully lift the ruler or card to avoid disturbing the pigment. Holding the brush vertically, paint in the castle using a watery mix of red and orange. Take the brushstrokes downwards towards the lower right corner and paint in the detailing at the top of the castle with the tip of the brush. Extend the painting outwards from the main tower.

10 Extend the painting out to the right and the left, gradually fading out the buildings and leaving just a suggestion of them.

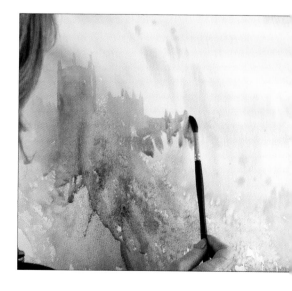

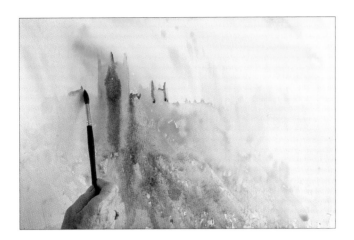

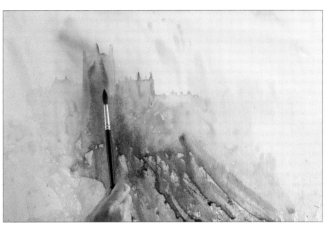

11 Splatter some turquoise paint into the foreground, then go in boldly with some darker colours to start to define the buildings, avoiding too much detail. Begin with heavily diluted violet, which can be a very strong pigment.

12 Start to inject more atmosphere into the foreground by splattering in turquoise, red then violet, and place a few directional brushstrokes moving away from the tower.

Tip
Give an illusion of movement through choice of techniques and directional lines.

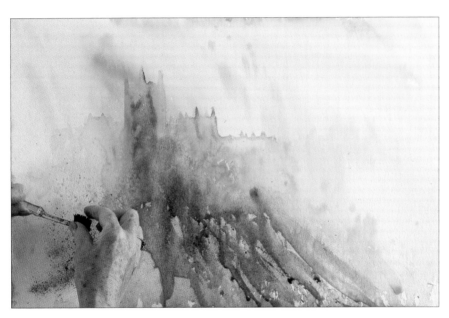

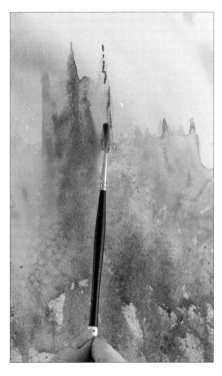

13 Splatter some water on to the top right of the painting to soften it and encourage the colour fusions to develop. Continue to build up the layers. Use the toothbrush to splatter more colour (red and purple) into the bottom left to add texture and interest, and to make it look different from the other corners of the painting. Splatter some turquoise over the main foreground too.

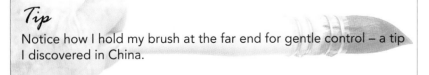

Tip
Notice how I hold my brush at the far end for gentle control – a tip I discovered in China.

14 Start to focus in on the main tower. Add more detail using dark purple on the walls of the building using the side of the brush. Change to the rigger to add finer detail.

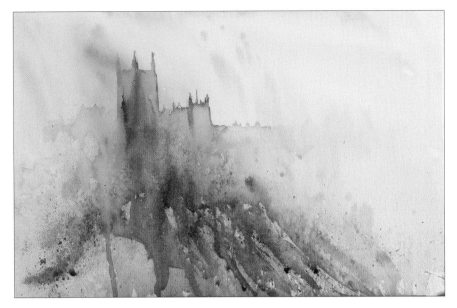

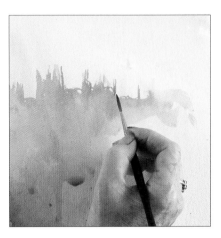

15 Strengthen the lower tower on the right, adding colour, then softening with a large, damp brush. This is a good point at which to stand back and assess your painting. Stop when you feel your painting is pleasing to the eye.

16 Extend the buildings out to the right using the size 10 brush, fading them into the sunlight. Add in a little purple, using a very watery mix. Change to the rigger to place a few hints of detail. Finally, splatter on some clean water to soften.

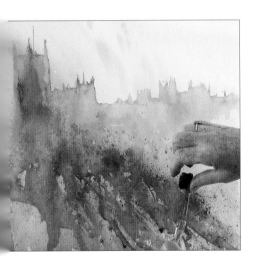

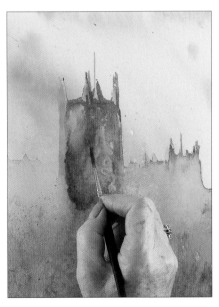

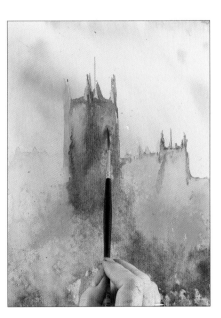

17 Paint in a staff on top of the main tower (use a ruler if you wish). Use purple to strengthen the tower still further and to suggest windows. Complete this stage by using a toothbrush to splatter on some colours from your palette. Finally, strengthen the colour in the lower right area of the painting with cadmium orange.

18 Decide if the main tower needs more detail. Using the rigger, put in the fourth, distant, turret. Gradually strengthen the outlines of the buildings. Soften some of the edges to create an illusion of misty morning sunlight.

19 Strengthen the buildings to the right where you feel further detail is needed. You can add some red on the right-facing wall of the main tower. Bleed the colour down into the lower areas of the painting.

Tip
Add impact by using unusual colour additions and strong contrasts of bold and soft colour.

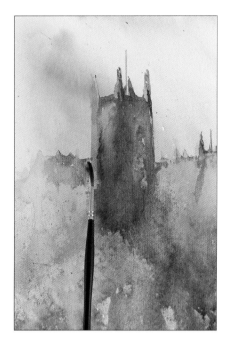

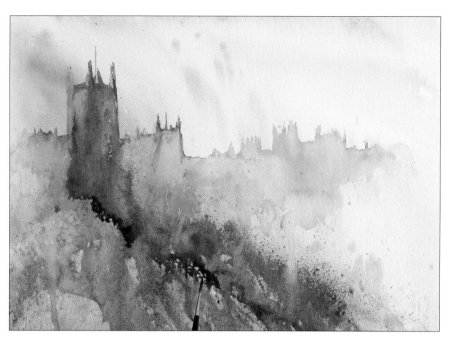

20 Strengthen the buildings on the left. Play with the colour contrasts, and soften the pigment as you work.

21 Taking the colour diagonally across the painting, look for the pattern created by the salt and accentuate it using alizarin crimson. Drop small amounts of perylene maroon into the wet alizarin crimson and allow it to fuse. This will create atmosphere within the painting.

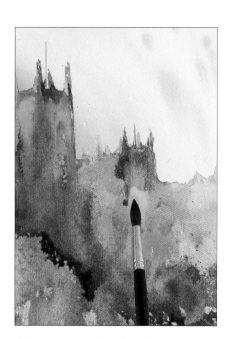

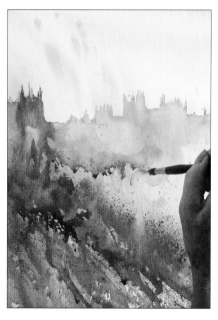

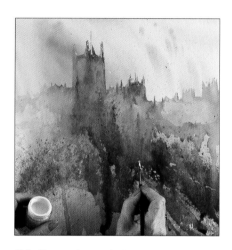

22 Load your brush with clean water and make a small, directional stroke on the distant tower. Leave to dry. This will give an illusion of light hitting the façade of the building.

23 Add a suggestion of a line of trees to the right of the main tower. You can splatter the foreground with turquoise to complete the picture. Allow to dry before applying the final highlights.

24 Once the painting is completely dry, apply tiny amounts of white gouache using the rigger to create points of light where the sunlight is striking the scene – at the tops of the buildings, and on the stones at the bottom of the picture. Use your imagination to create interest.

Tip
Don't overwork the highlights – a few carefully placed highlights can have a dramatic effect.

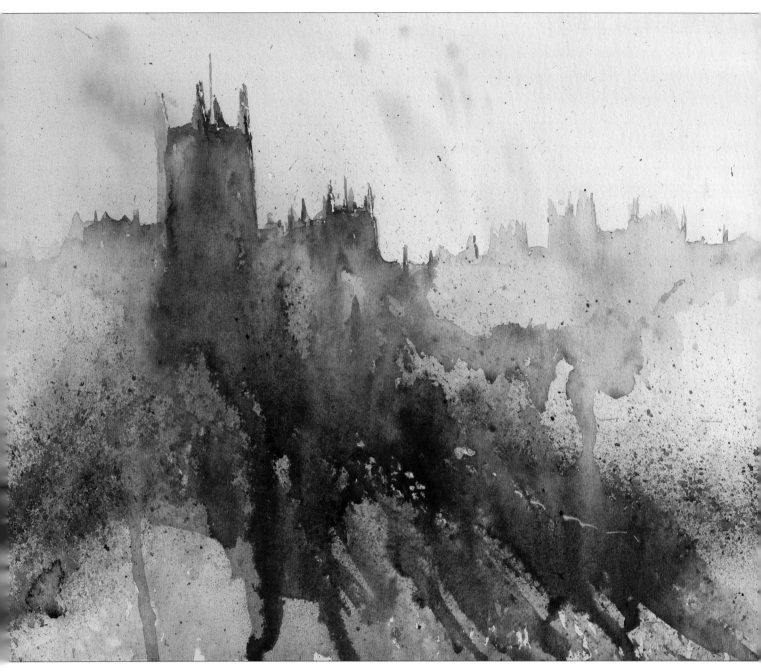

Celebration of Colour
56 x 38cm (22 x 15in)

Aim to create a painting that is full of intrigue, atmosphere, drama and
excitement. Allow the viewer to use their imagination to bring the scene to
life. Enjoy your experience of bringing the scene to life with glorious colour!

The Laird

Painting portraits without the use of a preliminary sketch, using a photograph for reference, can lead to unique and interesting results. Try looking at your subject and simply placing colour where you see shapes, leaving white areas to hint at light hitting the face. Have fun experimenting and, initially, don't worry too much about a likeness.

Either follow the steps below, using the finished painting on page 62 for reference, or create a portrait from a photograph of your own, using the project to guide you through the process.

The technique you will be using is direct painting – this means you begin with the subject rather than a background wash. You will need to work continually, therefore it is vital to mix ample colour before you start.

You will need

300gsm (140lb) rough watercolour paper, 38 x 56cm (15 x 22in)

Paintbrushes: size 8 squirrel pointed wash brush, and size 3 (fine rigger) and size 10 Kolinsky sable watercolour brushes

Palette

Watercolour paints: yellow ochre, perylene maroon, quinacridone gold, cadmium orange, alizarin crimson, sap green, Winsor violet, French ultramarine, cobalt turquoise

Designer's white gouache

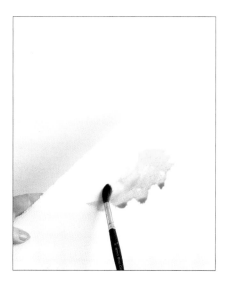

1 To achieve a flesh tone, start by making a watery mix of yellow ochre and alizarin crimson on your palette. Try out your mix on a spare piece of paper to obtain the correct tone. Adjust the mix until you are happy with the result.

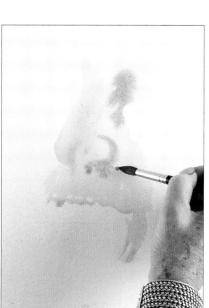

2 With the size 10 brush, hold the brush in the centre and start to paint the nose. Avoid definition at this stage. Using water, bleed the colour away from your starting point. As you work try to feel the shape of the face. Repeatedly refer to your chosen reference for guidance.

3 Introduce some alizarin crimson and play with the colour fusions to start adding definition to your painting. Drop in water at regular intervals to diffuse the pigment. Don't worry about drips – allow runs to develop.

> ### Tip
> Don't be afraid to experiment with colour early on in a painting. Drop water in regularly to spread out the pigment and produce effects you can play with later.

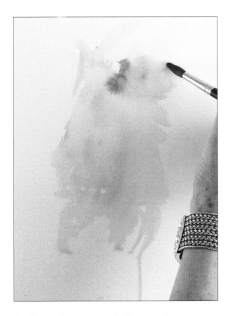

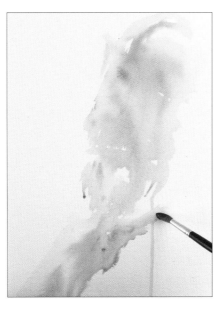

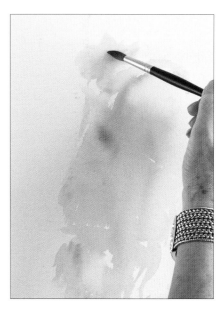

4 Bring in some violet and start to define the eye area above the nose. Don't be afraid to drop in colour at this stage – mistakes can be corrected later. Use the brush in different directions to 'mould' the subject. Remember we are only aiming at placing colour at this stage, not detail.

5 Continue to move towards the forehead. Next move in a downwards direction towards the beard. Layer turquoise over violet here. To move colour towards the lower left corner, lay a track of water then drop in alizarin crimson. Allow the pigment to flow along the water track.

6 Once the background washes are in place, you can start to add definition. Begin with the forehead. Place a water track with an upward curved brushstroke. Allow colour to merge into this track. Don't worry if you can't see the face yet – just work in colour sections.

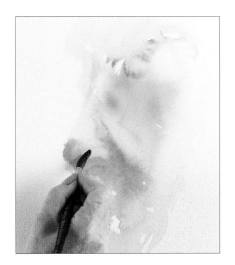

7 Turning your attention to the nose, begin to add some darker shades – perylene maroon, then alizarin crimson. Soften with water and encourage watermarks. Lift out the highlight on the nose using a damp brush and a curved brushstroke.

8 Define the moustache a little more, using purple applied with small, straight, downwards strokes. Put in a line of red where the mouth will be.

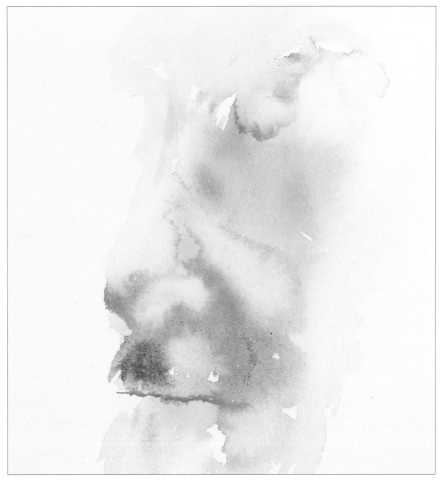

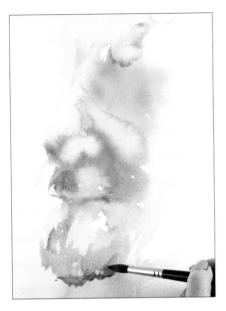

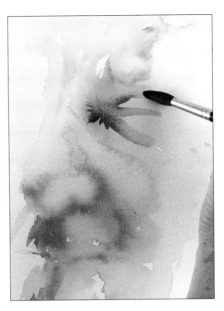

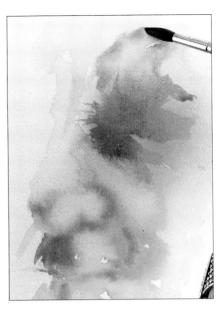

9 Working now on the beard, introduce violet, turquoise and then a little cadmium orange to warm and strengthen it. Start to add a little darker colour to define the lower edge.

10 Position the eye starting with a touch of violet. Bleed the colour away from the inner corner of the eye to define the socket. Work gently with the brush and 'feel' when the subject is beginning to appear.

11 Continue dropping soft colour in where you feel darks are needed. Work towards the eyebrow and forehead. Start looking for distinctive features, though at this stage continue building up the layers of colour only; avoid detail.

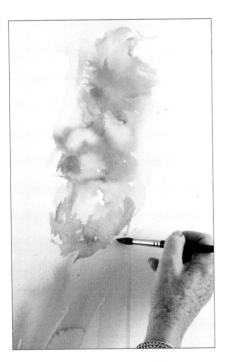

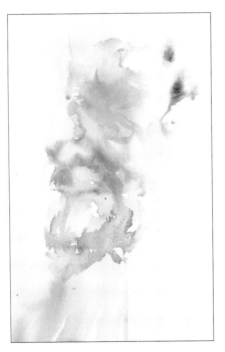

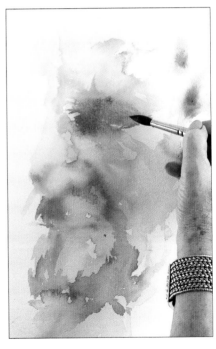

12 While the top part of the painting is drying, move down to the lower part of the face. Continue building up the colour in layers until the face starts to emerge. The more colour and pattern that develops, the more exciting the end result will be!

13 Introduce some cooler colours to the right of the head – this is where the sunlight is very strong, and shadows therefore more intense. Drop in turquoise followed by violet, which will create contrast. Lift out some colour to define the roundness of the cheek, and put in some stronger colour where you definitely know the cheek is.

14 Change to the small brush and find the eye using purple. Drop a little of the dark colour into the centre and pull it outwards to define the eye area. Add warmth to this area with a mixture of cadmium orange and alizarin crimson.

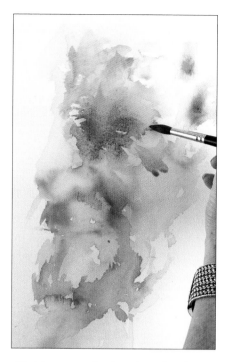

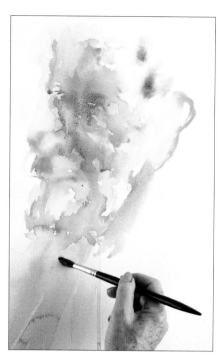

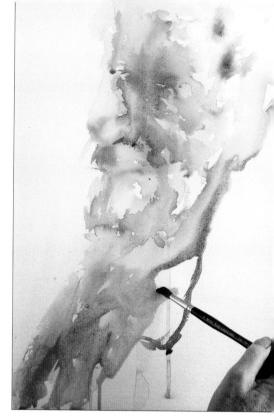

15 Mix some flesh colour for the area above the eye. While it is drying work on the upper cheek, bringing in some warm shades using curved brushstrokes.

16 Using quinacridone gold, define the ear and take the colour diagonally to the neck. Stop and look at your work frequently to see how your painting is developing.

17 Apply red at the base of the neck to suggest clothing, and around the back of the head. Drop some violet pigment into the damp alizarin crimson and allow it to merge. This will define the Laird's red cloak. Dropping in water will encourage patterns to form.

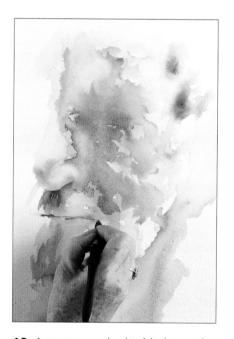

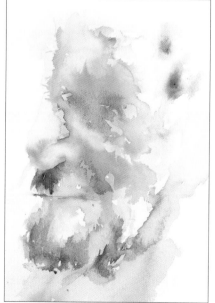

19 Continue building up the layers, gradually defining the main features to create character and capture the personality of your subject. Strengthen the turquoise in the lower part of the painting. This acts as a wonderful contrast with the warmer colours in your composition. Slightly darken the right-hand side of the beard using purple. Soften the colours as needed while you work. Accentuate the highlights by gently lifting out colour with a damp brush. You can strengthen the shadows under the nose at this stage if you wish.

18 Accentuate the highlight on the nose by building up the shadows underneath. Soften them slightly in places, then begin to strengthen the line of the mouth.

Tip
Work with the translucent properties of the individual pigments to enjoy the full benefit of the watercolour technique described as 'layering of colour', which is used in this demonstration.

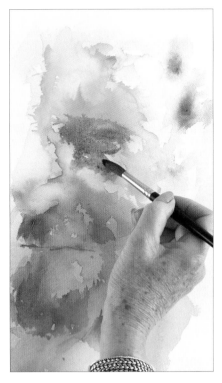

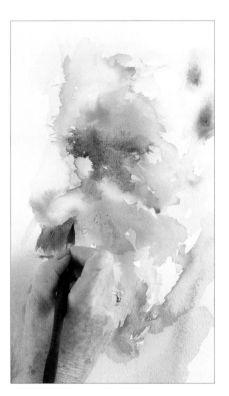

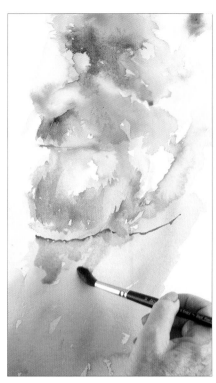

20 Put in the eye, aligning the inner corner with the edge of the nostril. Start by dropping in dark colour, then build up the detail. Work broadly around the eye area, then with clean water define the eye socket itself.

21 While the eye area is drying, work on other parts of the face that require further work – add some stronger colour to the top part of the face, drop in some alizarin crimson to warm up the cheek and darken the shadow under the nose.

22 Paint in the shadow area under the beard at the top of the neck using a mix of French ultramarine and sap green. Define the edge of the beard using an uneven line, then bleed the colour down. Drop a touch of the same colour under the nose to create harmony.

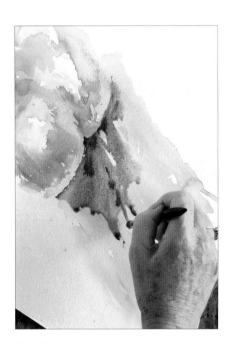

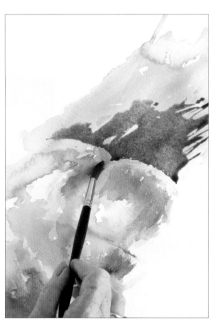

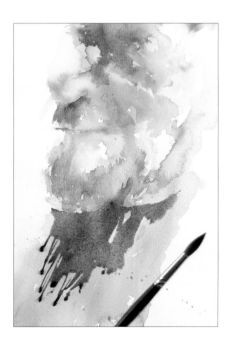

23 Turn the paper sideways, drop in some French ultramarine under the chin and let it run. Strengthen the shadow with a touch of violet.

24 Turn the painting upside down and wet the side of the beard, allowing colour from the neck to bleed into it. This marries the two areas together, creating harmony.

25 Turn the painting back up the right way and splatter in some orange to add more drama and contrast.

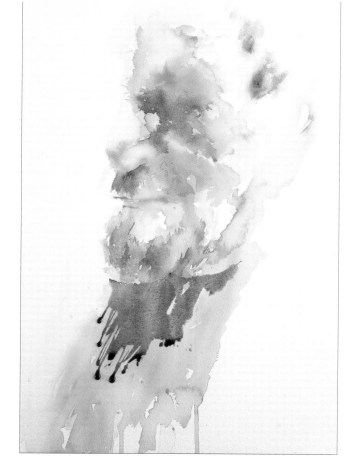

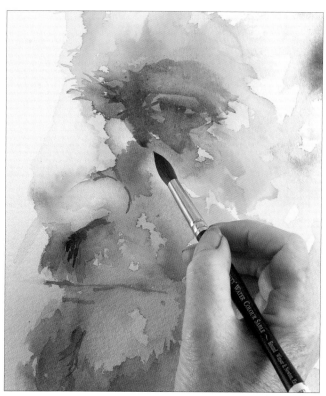

26 Add some further refinements to the painting using the rigger – enhance beard detail using fine brushstrokes with purple pigment. Indicate the lower lip with a soft brushstroke. Place some turquoise in the top right of the picture to balance the colour in the lower left. Add tiny creases at the top of the nose. Allow the painting to dry.

27 Start to add detail – define the curve of the nostril, and draw in the eye, beginning with the inner corner. Position it carefully, using your photograph or my finished painting for reference. Add colour to the eye socket, dampen and extend to the top of the cheek. Define the eyebrow and add some crease lines where needed.

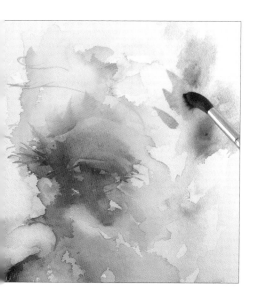

28 Place a few brushmarks on the side of the head to add character. Use the rigger to place some subtle fine lines across the forehead.

29 Complete the painting by adding sharp highlights using white gouache. Start at the top and bring in a few hints of hair, then gently lay the brush on the moustache and add one or two subtle highlights there. Next, use a mix of small and large brushstrokes to place highlights within the beard, then dot some on the bridge of the nose, on the curve of the nostril and just under the eyebrow. Soften the highlights with a little water.

Tip
Add impact to your paintings by using unusual colour additions with strong contrasts of bold and soft colour.

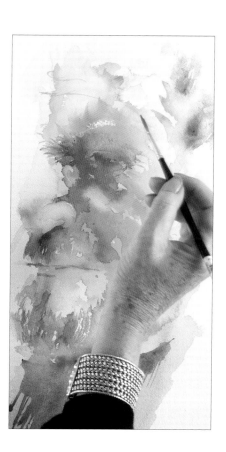

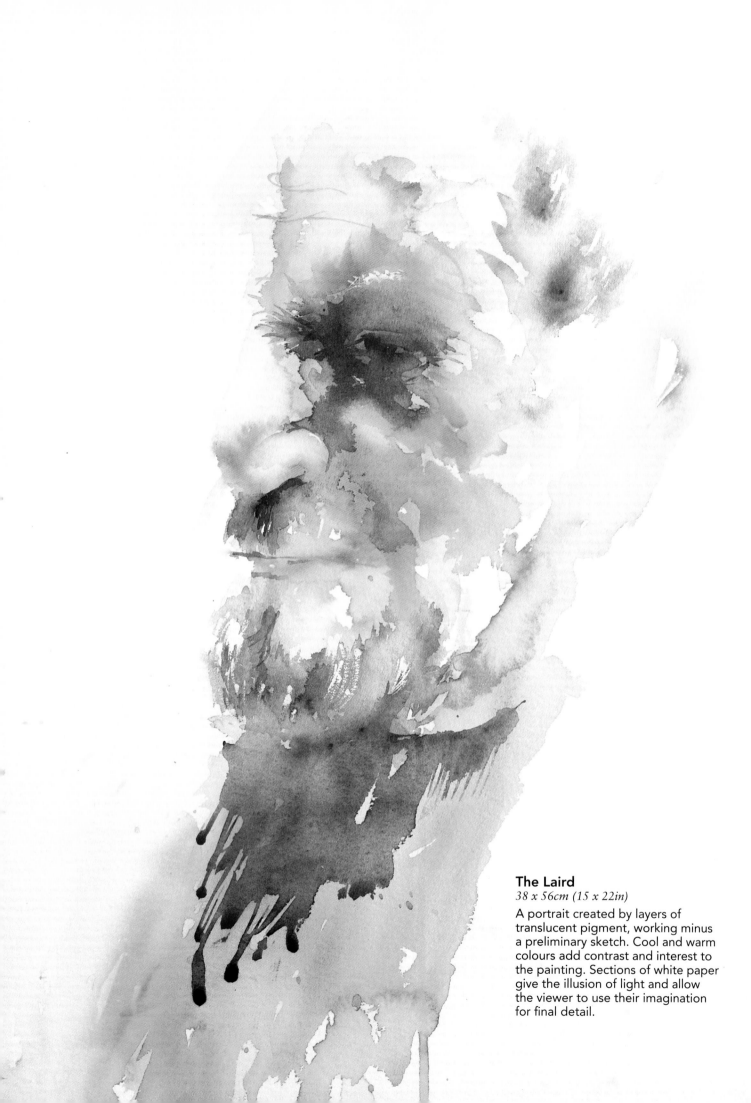

The Laird
38 x 56cm (15 x 22in)

A portrait created by layers of translucent pigment, working minus a preliminary sketch. Cool and warm colours add contrast and interest to the painting. Sections of white paper give the illusion of light and allow the viewer to use their imagination for final detail.

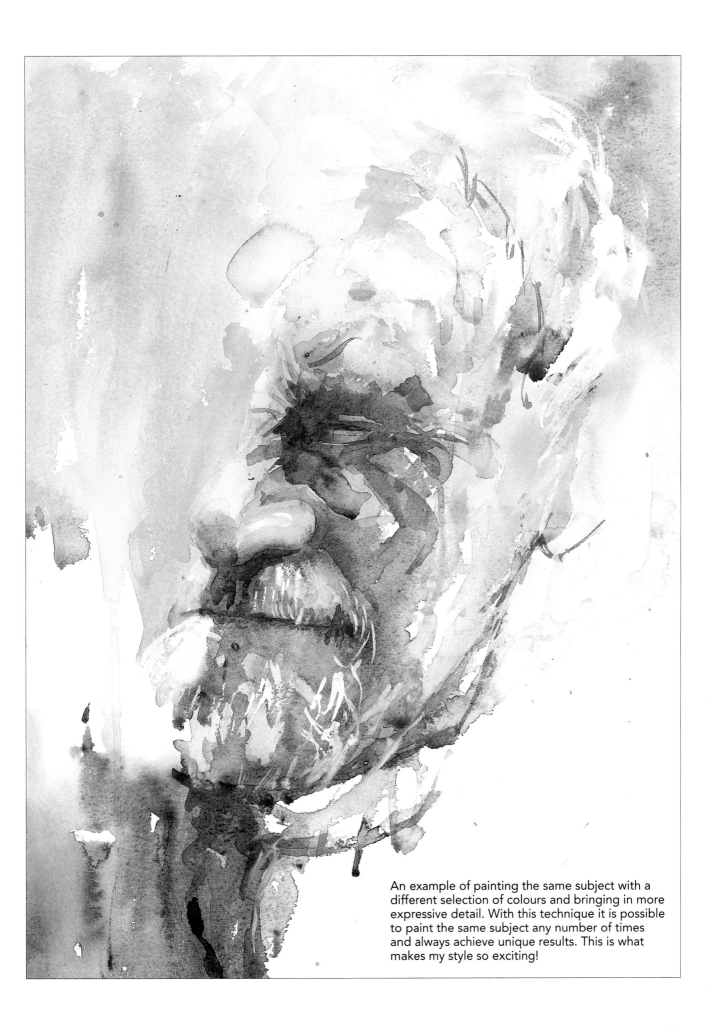

An example of painting the same subject with a different selection of colours and bringing in more expressive detail. With this technique it is possible to paint the same subject any number of times and always achieve unique results. This is what makes my style so exciting!

Index

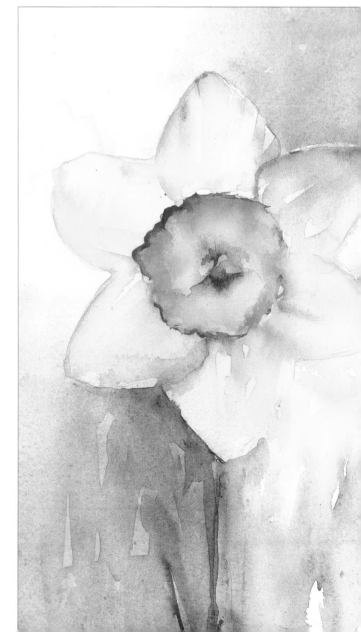

First Signs of Spring
25.5 x 30.5cm (10 x 12in)